VITTORIO SERRA

A DAY IN
FLORENCE

New Practical Guide of the Town

★ *152 colour illustrations*
★ *detailed map of the town*
★ *useful information*

26th edition - completely revised
1988/89 version

BONECHI · EDIZIONI «IL TURISMO»
Via dei Rustici, 5 · 50122 FLORENCE

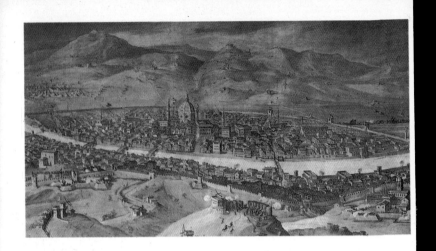

WELCOME TO FLORENCE!

You are about to explore this world-famous and seductive Romanesque, Gothic and Renaissance town, that has been sung by poets and lovers of beauty through the centuries. Successive building and alterations have not managed to disrupt the harmonious fabric of this town lovingly put together by laborious merchants and artists. City of the Lily, Birthplace of Dante, Cradle of the Renaissance, Town of the Medici: you will discover the many-coloured marble façades of numberless Romanesque and Gothic churches, the treasures in the museums, the chiselled, gilded or frescoed ceilings of the great halls in Palazzo Vecchio, Palazzo Pitti or Palazzo Strozzi, the austere grandeur of Florentine civic architecture. You will be entranced by the warm amber colours of the weathered sandstone (pietra forte) and of the terracotta, which give the whole town its lion-tawny tinge. You will wander along the alleys which still keep to the lines laid down by the old Roman "castrum's" founders, back in 59 B.C. and will come out on the Lungarni, to be dazzled by the pearly tints of the river Arno flowing beneath the deep arches of the Ponte Vecchio and Ponte Santa Trinita. Once across the bridges, you will be tempted to lean against the high parapets of the Lungarni to absorb the enchanting view of the battlemented towers and belfries of the old centre, etched dramatically and yet in such a familiar way against the flaming sunset sky.
Welcome, and happy wanderings in our company!

The Publisher

FIRST ITINERARY

Piazza del Duomo - Baptistry - Giotto's Bell Tower - Cathedral - Cathedral Museum - Palazzo Medici-Riccardi - San Lorenzo - Laurentian Library - Medici Chapels

Aerial view of the Cathedral, Baptistery and Belltower.

PIAZZA DEL DUOMO

At the dawn of the Middle Ages, the site of the Piazza was a mass of dwelling houses and public buildings. The church of Santa Reparata was built over the foundations of one of the latter in the 4th century. Three centuries later (though some think in the same century) the Baptistry was built next to the church, and this area began to be the centre of religious life in Florence. Santa Reparata became a cathedral in 1128. The church was becoming too small for its new role and increased importance — the

3

population was increasing too — and in 1289 the Commune decided to enlarge it. This was part of an extensive rebuilding project, involving new and more extensive city walls (the Roman circle was too small), the construction of a Priors' Palace (now Palazzo Vecchio) and alterations to existing buildings such as Santa Croce, the church of the Badia, Orsanmichele, the Bargello and the Baptistry. In order to achieve a city that should be new but harmonious, one man, Arnolfo di Cambio, was given the responsibility of directing and coordinating the work. One of the greatest architects and sculptors of his time, he raised the level of the piazza (which he had re-paved), eliminating the podium on which the Baptistry previously stood, demolished a few houses nearby, and began to build the new cathedral, for which he planned a dome and external decoration matching that of the Baptistry. The death of Arnolfo in 1302 put a stop to the work, which was resumed in 1332-34 with the construction of the belltower under the direction of Giotto. The addition of a dome by Brunelleschi (1420-36) made it the impressive, dominating building that we see today.

BAPTISTRY

Dante's "Bel San Giovanni" (Fair St. John) the religious building most beloved by the Florentines, was perhaps started in the 7th century, but the work done in the 11th-12th centuries made it the most important monument of Romanesque architecture in Florence. Its regular octagonal form and the symmetrical distribution of the external decoration were, for centuries, an architectural ideal for artists of the stature of Arnolfo, Giotto, Brunelleschi, Leon Battista Alberti, Leonardo and Michelangelo. It has three magnificent bronze doors. The **South Door** is by Andrea Pisano (c. 1330): it consists of 28 panels illustrating the *Life of the Baptist*; the bronze cornice is by Vittorio Ghiberti (son of Lorenzo, 1452). The **North Door** is by Lorenzo Ghiberti, cast betwen 1403-1424, after winning a competition in which Brunelleschi also took part; the 28 panels represent *episodes from the Life of Christ*. The East Door, the famous "**door of Paradise**", is also by Lorenzo Ghiberti (1425-1452); it is composed of 10 gilded bronze panels, with complex *Scenes from the Old Testament*, crowded with figures. The smooth pyramidal roof-covering is topped by a lantern. The **inside** of the Baptistry, like the outside, is on an octagonal plan with marble decoration and each wall divided into three by tall columns; the twin-arched windows of the women's gallery open above the trabeation. A baptismal font, mentioned by Dante in the *Divine Comedy*, used to stand in the centre of the fine inlaid marble floor but was removed in the 16th century by Buontalenti, by order of the Grand Duke Francesco I. Against the

The Baptistry of St. John seen from the south side of Piazza del Duomo.

wall are a *baptismal font* of the Pisan school, 14th century; the *tomb of the anti-Pope John XXIII*, the work of Donatello and Michelozzo, commissioned by the banker Giovanni dei Medici, two Roman sarcophagi and a 13th century altar. The beautiful and very striking wooden statue of Mary *Magdalen* by Donatello (1435-55), which used to be in the Baptistry, is now on view in the Cathedral Museum. The interior of the vault is covered by

Creation of Adam and Eve. – Original sin. – Expulsion from Paradise.

Story of Noah: Noah's family leaves the ark after the Flood. – Noah gives thanks to the Lord who sends a rainbow as a sign of peace. – Drunkenness of Noah. – Noah is derided by Ham and covered up by Shem and Japhet.

Story of Jacob and Esau: Esau trades his birthright for a plate of lentils. – Isaac sends Esau hunting. – Jacob throws a goat's skin around his neck. – Isaac mistakes Jacob for Esau and gives him his blessing. – Jacob leaves his father's house.

Lorenzo Ghiberti

Story of Moses: Moses receives the Tablets of the Law on Mount Sinai. – Aaron waits halfway down the mountain. – The Hebrews, terrified by the thunder and lightning, await Moses' return at the foot of the mountain.

Story of Saul and David: Saul defeats the Philistines. – David smites Goliath. – David carries Goliath's head before the cheering crowd, back to Jerusalem.

The Door

of Paradise.

Adam and Eve, Cain and Abel. – Abel keeping sheep and Cain ploughing. – Cain kills Abel. – Curse of Cain.

Story of Abraham: Sarah at the entrance to the tent. – Apparition of the angels to Abraham. – Abraham and Isaac on the mountain. – The Angel stays Abraham's hand as he is about to sacrifice Isaac.

Story of Joseph: Joseph is sold to the merchants and brought before Pharaoh. – Interpretation of Pharaoh's dream. – The golden cup in Benjamin's bag. – Joseph reveals himself to his brothers and forgives them. – Joseph meets Jacob.

Vittorio Ghiberti

Story of Joshua: Joshua and the Hebrews cross the Jordan and crowd before the Ark. – The Hebrews gather twelve stones for commemoration. – The walls of Jericho fall at the sound of the Angels' trumpets.

King Solomon ceremoniously receives the Queen of Sheba in the Temple of Jerusalem.

Left: the northern door by L. Ghiberti; *right:* the southern door, by Andrea Pisano; *below:* interior of the Baptistry.

The mosaics on the Baptistry vault, with the Last Judgement.

mosaics laid between the mid-13th and the mid-14th century by local and Venetian craftsmen (in the Middle Ages Venice was the greatest centre for mosaics). The most important artists who made the cartoons for the mosaics include Cimabue (*Scenes from the life of Joseph*) and Coppo di Marcovaldo (*Christ*). The subjects of the magnificent design are *Scenes from the Old and New Testament* and the *Last Judgment*, dominated by the impressive figure of the *Judging Christ*.

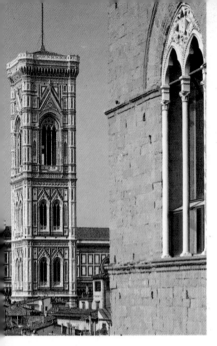

Left: **Giotto's Belltower;** *right*: **the Loggia del Bigallo.**

GIOTTO'S BELL TOWER

The building of this tower began in 1334 under the direction of Giotto, after a fire had destroyed the old bell-tower of Santa Reparata. Giotto died in 1337, when the base of the tower had been completed; after him work was directed by Andrea Pisano and Francesco Talenti, who brought it to conclusion (although the original plan included a spire which was never built). The building is of remarkable grace and elegance; the structure lightens and lengthens as it rises, becoming complex with marble insets and fine perforation. The bas-reliefs on the base (the originals are in the Cathedral Museum) were carved by Andrea Pisano and his workmen under the supervision of Giotto.

Next to the bell tower, on the corner of Via Calzaioli, the graceful **Loggia del Bigallo**, built between 1352 and 1358 by Alberto Arnoldi, in elegant Gothic style, as a shelter for the town's waifs and orphans (Innocents). Its façade, facing the Baptistry, has three tabernacles with the statues of *St. Peter the Martyr*, the *Virgin and Child* and *St. Luke*. Inside is a fine collection of works of art, with frescoes detached from the building and works by Ghirlandaio, Arnoldi and the schools of Botticelli and Verrocchio.

Overall view of the Cathedral or Duomo.

CATHEDRAL

The construction of the Cathedral, dedicated to Santa Maria del Fiore (St. Mary of the Flower) was begun in 1294 by Arnolfo di Cambio, chosen by the city authorities and the citizens, who wanted a cathedral not only larger than the previous church of Santa Reparata but "so sumptuous and magnificent" that it would outshine the cathedrals of rival Tuscan cities both in beauty and dimensions. The new cathedral was constructed around the older church, whose simple structure and two bell-towers were incorporated. Santa Reparata was finally pulled down in 1375; but the Florentines went on calling the new cathedral by the old name for a long time — the authorities had to inflict heavy fines in order to enforce the use of the new one: "Santa Maria del Fiore". The lower part of **Santa Reparata**, buried underneath the floor of the Duomo till quite recently, can now be visited by going down a staircase from the right aisle; it contains remains of frescoes, sculptures and tombstones, including that of Filippo Brunelleschi. The stately and spacious **interior** of the Duomo was the scene of the fiery sermons of Savonarola, and of the savage Pazzi conspiracy: on April 26th 1478 members of the Pazzi family, enemies of the Medicis, in league with Archbishop Salviati, attacked Lorenzo the

The façade of the Cathedral.

Interior of the Cathedral.

Magnificent and his brother Giuliano during Easter Day Mass. Lorenzo escaped, but Giuliano was killed and the conspiracy was followed by harsh repression. Works of art of many centuries embellish the cathedral but do not mask the severity of its high ogival arches and composite pillars. On the inside of the façade is an enormous clock, painted in 1443 and decorated with four heads of *Prophets* painted by Paolo Uccello. Also by Paolo Uccello is the fresco of the *Monument to Giovanni Acuto* (John Hawkwood) on the wall in the left aisle; beside, left, is the *Monument to Niccolò da Tolentino*, by Andrea del Castagno (1456). Above the large octagonal tribune is the **dome** by Brunelleschi. A competition for the construction of the cupola was announced in 1418. The difficulty of this task was immediately evident, for traditional building techniques were inadequate. Brunelleschi invented an original system of mobile centres which superseded the usual one of fixed structures starting from the ground (clearly impossible to use owing to the enormous dimensions of the building) and so succeeded in defeating Lorenzo Ghiberti, his eternal rival, who also took part in the competition. The dome and the lantern were completed in 1436. The dome is based on a massive octagonal drum, has marble ribbing and is covered by red tiles baked in the kilns at Impruneta. The inside of the dome is decorated with frescoes by Giorgio Vasari and Federico Zuccari (1572-79) representing the *Last Judgment* in five superimposed bands. Over the high altar is a wooden *Crucifix* by Benedetto da Maiano; and

Left: Niccolò da Tolentino, by A. del Castagno; *right*: John Hawkwood (Giovanni Acuto), by Paolo Uccello; *below*: grave stones in Santa Reparata (Cathedral).

View of the Cathedral Apse.

round it is the octagonal **choir** by Baccio Bandinelli (1555), decorated with bas-reliefs. Behind the altar on the right is the **Old Sacristy** with an *Ascension* in terracotta by Luca della Robbia in the lunette over the entrance. Directly opposite on the other side of the Tribune is the **New Sacristy**, with a fine bronze door by Luca della Robbia, Michelozzo and Maso di Bartolomeo (1445-69). In the lunette, *Resurrection*, also by Luca. Inside the sacristy, splendid 15th century *inlaid cupboards*. In the chapel at the end of the apse is a bronze urn by Ghiberti with relics of Saint Zanobius.

The Donatello and Luca della Robbia Room in the Museo dell'Opera del Duomo.

CATHEDRAL MUSEUM

Situated behind the Cathedral, the museum contains works from the Cathedral, the Bell-Tower and Baptistry. A room on the ground floor houses the sculptures from the first façade of the Cathedral, demolished in 1587, with a splendid *Virgin and Child* by Arnolfo di Cambio. The next room contains building material and mechanical devices used by Brunelleschi when building the dome. Another small room has a collection of precious reliquaries. The famous **Pietà** (*Deposition*) by Michelangelo is on the mezzanine.

The seventy-eight year-old sculptor used a capital that came from an ancient Roman temple for this group, which he hoped to use as his own grave monument in a chapel he owned in Santa Maria Maggiore in Rome. On the floor above: the two *choir balconies* by Donatello and Luca della Robbia; the Andrea Pisano *marble panels* from the bell tower; the statues of the *Baptist*, *Mary Magdalen* and *Abacuc* by Donatello. Donatello's strongly realistic style in the statues of the prophets for the bell tower becomes astoundingly and exasperatedly tragic in his unique wooden Mary Magdalen. She is not the traditionally youthful beauty, which we find in most Florentine representations of the Saint, but a repentant old woman, a macabre and horrifying apparition of a being consumed by vice, sinful living and sufferings. See also the

Left: **the wooden statue of Mary Magdalen, by Donatello;** *right*: **the famous Michelangelo Pietà or Deposition** (Museo dell'Opera).

beautiful *silver altar* of the Baptistery, by Michelozzo, Pollaiolo, Verrocchio and others.

We turn right as we leave the museum and walk back towards the Cathedral façade. At the corner we turn right into **via Martelli**. Lined with fine shops and important book stores, this is one of Florence's busiest thoroughfares. A short way up, on the lefthand side, we come to the **church of San Giovannino**. Across the street on the same side is the renowned Medici-Riccardi Palace.

Palazzo Medici-Riccardi.

PALAZZO MEDICI - RICCARDI

Built for Cosimo the Elder, between 1444 and 1460, by the Florentine architect and sculptor Michelozzo Michelozzi, this was the prototype of all Florentine palaces of the Renaissance. Majestic and elegant, it was filled with works of art commissioned by the Medici: the main branch of the family lived here until 1540. In 1655 the palace was sold to the Riccardi family and is now the seat of the provincial administration and the Prefecture. Exhibitions and other cultural events often take place here. It was designed by Michelozzo as a large cube, and must have stood out among the lower buildings round it; but the Riccardi family had it enlarged, adding seven new windows on Via Larga (now Via Cavour). The two principal sides, have pronounced rustication on the ground floor, flatter rustication on the storey above and smooth stones on the third. This motif was to reappear frequently

Detail from the Cavalcade of the Magi, by B. Gozzoli (Palazzo Medici Riccardi).

for more than a century, along with the use of twin-arched mullioned windows. There is a fine classical cornice, while the big corner windows (called "kneeling windows" from the form of the corbels) which replaced a previously existing loggia, are attributed to Michelangelo (c. 1517). On the same corner is a large Medici coat of arms. Inside the palace is a fine porticoed **courtyard**, that contains Roman remains and various pieces of sculpture. This palace used to contain many of the masterpieces that are now on view in the galleries and museums of Florence. One of the most important items is the **Chapel** by Michelozzo, at the top of the first staircase on the right from the courtyard. Here are the celebrated frescoes by Benozzo Gozzoli representing the *Journey of the Three Kings to Bethlehem* (1459-60) in which many personages of the time are portrayed: Lorenzo the Magnificent with his father, Piero the Gouty and his sisters; Galeazzo Maria Sforza; Sigismondo Malatesta; John VII Paleologus, Emperor of Constantinople; the painter himself and his master, Fra Angelico.

There is also an interesting **Gallery**, reached by going up the second staircase on the right, from the courtyard, decorated with stuccoes and mirrors at the end of the 18th century, with a fine frescoed ceiling by Luca Giordano showing the *Apotheosis of the Medici dynasty* (1682-83).

After leaving the palace, the short Via dei Gori, flanking the building to one's right, leads into **Piazza San Lorenzo** — a picturesque and lively market square, dominated by the cumbersome bulk of the church of San Lorenzo with the Chapel of the Princes' dome behind it. The monument to **Giovanni dalle Bande Nere**, by Baccio Bandinelli (1540) stands at the Via dei Gori corner of the square.

The Basilica of San Lorenzo and the market all around it.

SAN LORENZO

An ancient basilica, consecrated in 393 by St. Ambrose, bishop of Milan, it was probably the first church to be built on Florentine ground. Rebuilt in the 11th century, it was radically restored in the 15th century for the Medicis, for whom it was the family church. The **interior**, spacious, light and elegant, is an early Florentine Renaissance masterpiece; it was designed by Brunelleschi in 1420 and he directed the work from 1442 until his death in 1446. It is in the form of a Latin cross and has a nave and two aisles with side chapels. There are numerous masterpieces,

Interior of the Basilica of San Lorenzo.

including two **bronze pulpits** by Donatello at the end of the nave, the master's last work (about 1440), completed after his death by pupils; a fine marble tabernacle by Desiderio da Settignano (mid 15th century) opposite the pulpit on the right; the *Marriage of the Virgin*, a painting by Rosso Fiorentino (1523) in the second chapel on the right; a remarkable *Annunciation*, with *Scenes of the life of St. Nicholas of Bari* by Filippo Lippi (c. 1440) in the predella, in the left chapel of the left transept: also a large fresco representing the *Martyrdom of St. Laurence* by Bronzino (1565-69) in the left aisle, opposite the pulpit. Finally, the **Old Sacristy**, exceptionally important for its architecture and works of art, is off the left transept. Elegant and of crystalline simplicity in its spatial conception, it fully expresses Brunelleschi's architectural ideal (1420-29). The eight fine tondi in the lunettes and pendentives (4 with *Scenes from the life of St. John the Evangelist* and 4 with the *Evangelists*) are by Donatello, as are the two bronze doors beside the altar and a fine clay bust of *St. Laurence*; in the centre of the chapel, under a large marble table, is the *tomb of Giovanni di Bicci dei Medici and Piccarda Bueri*, the parents of Cosimo the Elder, by Andrea Cavalcanti (1434); on the left wall, under a large arch, is the *Tomb of Piero the Gouty and Giovanni dei Medici*, sons of Cosimo the Elder, by Andrea del Verrocchio, helped probably by Leonardo.

LAURENTIAN LIBRARY

The entrance is at No. 9, piazza San Lorenzo. Across the lovely **cloister** by Manetti, a pupil of Brunelleschi, the stairs in the right corner lead up to the Library commissioned by Clement VII in 1524, designed by Michelangelo and completed around 1578. It contains the magnificent collection of manuscripts, incunabola and codices amassed by Cosimo the Elder and the Magnificent Lorenzo such as the Medici *Virgil* (4th-5th century), the *Pandects of Justinian* (6th century), the oldest existing examples of the *tragedies of Aeschylus* (11th century) as well as of the writings of *Thucidides, Herodotus* and *Tacitus* (10th century). The **Vestibule** was designed by Michelangelo and Ammannati. The reading room terracotta floor echoes the cedar-wood ceiling design by Tribolo, another follower of Michelangelo.

The entrance to the Medici Chapels is behind the church.

MEDICI CHAPELS

The mausoleum of the Medicis contains seven statues by Michelangelo. Inside, there is first a wide crypt, which leads up to the sumptuous **Princes' Chapel**, ordered by Ferdinando I in 1602. Work began two years later upon a plan by Matteo Nigetti, and Buontalenti, and continued for more than a century. The great octagonal space is lined with inlaid semi-precious stone wall-panels of spectacular effect. Against the walls are the sarcophagi of six Medici grand dukes; above those of Ferdinando I and Cosimo II, statues in gilt bronze by Ferdinando Tacca; below: the sixteen coats of arms of Tuscan cities, in inlaid semi-precious stones; the high altar, covered with marble and semi-precious stones, is a modern reconstruction, with pieces originating in various periods. The frontal has a representation of the *Supper at Emmaus*. The chapel-dome is frescoed with *Scenes from the Old and New Testament*, by Pietro Benvenuti (1828). A corridor leads to the **New Sacristy**, the famous and beautiful chapel built by Michelangelo for Cardinal Giulio de' Medici, later Pope Clement VII. Michelangelo worked on it, through various vicissitudes, from 1520 until his patron, who had given him a completely free hand, died and he left Florence for good (1534). The chapel was never finished. On a square plan, it resembles the structure of Brunelleschi's Old Sacristy, but with much richer and more complex architectural decoration (niches, windows, arches etc.). The only complete tombs are those of two minor members of the great Florentine family; Giuliano, Duke of Nemours, and Lorenzo, Duke of Urbino, son of Piero the Unfortunate. The two tombs, facing each other, are placed on either side of the altar, in a splendid architectural setting of white marble and grey sand-stone (pietra serena). The idealised figures of the two young men in Roman

Left: the Chapel of the Princes; *right* the Arms of Florence in inlaid semi-precious stones.

dress and armour sit above the two sarcophagi. *Giuliano*, Duke of Nemours' tomb is on the right, looking at the altar, with reclining figures of *Night* (a gleaming, polished moon-like female figure sunk in sleep) and *Day* (a relaxed, muscular male figure, whose deliberately unfinished features half-concealed behind his power-ful hunched shoulder evoke the sun rising behind a mist-shrouded mountain) at each end of his sarcophagus.

Lorenzo, duke of Urbino is sunk in thought (he has in fact been nick-named "Il Pensieroso" – "the Thinker"). The reclining figures on his sarcophagus represent *Dawn* (a newly awakened girl, stretching herself voluptuously) and *Dusk* (a weary old man, whose grey exhaustion seems to have eaten away his fading features). The curving volutes surmounting the two urns sym-bolically enable the souls of the two dukes to flee the confines of space and time, to attain the transcendental domain of Eternity. Above the sarcophagus containing the remains of Lorenzo the Magnificent and his brother Giuliano, killed in the Pazzi conspir-acy, is the beautiful *Virgin and Child*, also by Michelangelo, at which the two dukes gaze; at the sides, *St. Cosmas* (left) by Montorsoli and *St. Damian* (right) by Raffaello da Montelupo, works by two pupils of Michelangelo that fall far below the expressive achievement of the statues near them. This work by Michelangelo, though unfinished, is generally interpreted as a

Above: **Interior of the Chapel of the Princes;** *below:* **detail of the Supper at Emmaus, on the altar front in the Chapel of the Princes.** (Medici Chapels).

lofty meditation on human destiny, its vanity and its redemption by religious faith. The three zones of the chapel can be understood in this sense: the lower order, with the tombs and allegorical statues, represents all-consuming Time that leads inexorably to death, to Hades; the middle band is the terrestrial sphere, and the upper one, more luminous, with the lunettes and the dome, the vault of Heaven.

Above: **Interior of the New Sacristy;** *below*: **detail of the coffered vault of the dome** (Medici Chapels).

25

Interior of Orsanmichele.

ORSANMICHELE

The religious and civic centres of Florence, Piazza del Duomo and
Piazza della Signoria, are connected by **Via Calzaioli**, an elegant,
busy shopping street, where the square bulk of Orsanmichele,
originally intended as a market, was subsequently converted into
a church. In 1284 the Florentine republic appointed Arnolfo to
build a loggia for the collection and storage of grain, in the garden
(orto) of the Monastery of San Michele — hence the name. This
was burnt down in 1304, and rebuilt between 1337 and 1404 by
Francesco Talenti and Neri di Fioravante in the elegant, "decorated" Gothic style. The deposits were on the two upper floors, the
grain flowed down to the loggia of the grain market below
through the chutes in the pillars and out of the still visible
openings (inside the church). The external decoration was con-
tracted out to the various city Guilds; each had a tabernacle with

The Wool Guild Hall (Palazzo dell'Arte della Lana).

its coat of arms and the statue of its patron saint. Remarkable, among the sculptures, are: the *Baptist* and *St. Matthew* by Ghiberti, *St. George* by Donatello (original in the Bargello) and the classical *Four Crowned Saints* by Nanni di Banco. The interior has a double nave with high cross vaults; in the right one, *tabernacle* by Andrea Orcagna (1359), a large Gothic cusped shrine, whose base is decorated with bas-reliefs of *Scenes of the life of the Virgin* and which contains the *Madonna of Mercies*, by Bernardo Daddi.

Linked to Orsanmichele by a covered bridge, built to Cosimo I's orders, connecting the first storeys of the two buildings, is the **Palazzo dell'Arte della Lana** (Wool Guild Hall), one of the most important guilds in Medieval Florence. Started in 1308, it underwent various transformations over the centuries. In 1905 it was restored by Enrico Lusini and the fine frescoed rooms became the seat of the Dante Society. The 14th century *Gothic Tabernacle of the Madonna of the Trumpet* on the corner of Via dell'Arte della Lana and Via Orsanmichele has a *Madonna* by Jacopo del Casentino.

Aerial view of Piazza della Signoria.

PIAZZA DELLA SIGNORIA

Via Calzaioli ends in Piazza della Signoria. In Roman times, the area that is now the civic centre of the town was occupied by dwelling houses and the theatre. At the end of the 13th century, the area was included in the town-planning scheme directed by Arnolfo di Cambio, who requisitioned and pulled down the houses of Ghibelline families standing there and began to build Palazzo Vecchio. Henceforward the piazza became the setting for public

Detail from the **terrible Death of Savonarola** (panel in the Museum of St. Mark's).

speeches, ceremonies, meetings, uproars, executions: famous, especially, that of **Gerolamo Savonarola**, the preacher who was, for a short time, the arbiter of political life in the city and was excommunicated and burnt at the stake as a heretic on May 23rd, 1498, on the spot now indicated by a plaque in front of the Neptune Fountain. The Gothic loggia was built in the 14th century. On the side opposite the Loggia, at N° 5, is the **Alberto della Ragione collection** (works of contemporary Italian art) and at N° 7, **Palazzo Uguccioni**, built to a design by Michelangelo or Raphael, and on the east side the **Tribunal of the Guilds**, built in 1359.

The Loggia of the Signoria during the annual Flower Market.

LOGGIA DEI LANZI

This is also called the Loggia della Signoria because it was built to shelter the public ceremonies of the Signoria; or also the Loggia dell'Orcagna from the name of the architect who, according to Vasari, designed it. The Lanzi were the Lanzichenecchi (Lands-knechts), German mercenaries in the pay of Cosimo I, who used the Loggia as their bivouac for a certain period. The Loggia was built between 1376 and 1383 by Benci di Cione and Simone Talenti. It consists of three large classical arches, supported by composite pillars and a spacious cross-vaulted porch. The lobed panels between the arches were carved between 1384 and 1389 upon designs by Agnolo Gaddi and enclose statues of the *Virtues*.Two heraldic *lions* flank the entrance: the one on the right is an ancient Roman statue, the other is 16th century. Under the right arch is the *Rape of the Sabines*, by Giambologna (1583), a work of refined virtuosity, which introduces the Baroque and was prin-cipally conceived to present and solve novel technical and compositional problems, wherefore it only received its name after it was finished. The left arch frames the *Perseus* by Benvenuto Cellini (1546-54): the hero holding up the head of Medusa has a classical stateliness and an almost Manneristic grace; the base is

The Rape of the Sabines, by Giambologna and the Perseus, by
B. Cellini.

Hercules and the Centaur, by Giambologna and the Abduction of Polyxena, by Pio Fedi.

splendid, with statues and bas-reliefs that reveal the artist's skill as a goldsmith. The loggia also contains *Hercules and Nessus*, another group by Giambologna, *Menelaus bearing the body of Patrocles*, a Roman copy of a Greek original of the 4th century B.C.; *six Roman female statues* and the *Abduction of Polixena*, a fine work by the nineteenth century sculptor Pio Fedi.

NEPTUNE FOUNTAIN

Bartolomeo Ammannati was architect to Grand Duke Cosimo. He designed the courtyard of Pitti Palace, the Carraia and Santa Trinita bridges and worked on numerous mansions all over Florence; as a sculptor, his most important work is this fountain in the piazza, commissioned by Cosimo and sculpted between 1563 and 1576. In the centre of the polygonal pool is the large figure of *Neptune* (whose bearded features recall the artist's patron, Cosimo), standing on a coach drawn by sea-horses; all round the edge of the pool the magnificent bronze figures of *Naiads*, *Tritons* and *Satyrs* reveal the hand of Giambologna, Ammannati's assistant.

The Neptune Fountain, by Ammannati; *below*: two bronze naiads from the rim of the fountain.

The Equestrian Monument to Cosimo I de' Medici, by Giambologna; *opposite*: **Palazzo della Signoria or Palazzo Vecchio.**

On the steps of the Palace: the *Marzocco*, the lion of the Florentine republic, a copy of Donatello's original, now in the Bargello; a copy of Michelangelo's *David*; now in the Academy, placed here in 1504; *Hercules and Cacus* by Bandinelli (1534) and two statuettes (perhaps *Philemon* and *Baucis* changed into plants) by De' Rossi and Bandinelli. Opposite the fountain is an imposing *equestrian monument to Cosimo I de' Medici* by Giambologna (1954). The reliefs around the base represent: *The Tuscan Senate confering the title of grandduke on Cosimo I* (1537), *Pius V presenting Cosimo with the insignia of the rank of grandduke* (1569), and *Cosimo victoriously entering Siena* (1557). Donatello's *Judith and Holophernes* formerly on the steps of the palace is at present being restored.

PALAZZO VECCHIO

Palazzo della Signoria, called Palazzo Vecchio, the old palace, after the middle of the 15th century when the Medici left it and moved to Palazzo Pitti, has always been the seat of the city's highest political authorities, (The Municipal council still has its offices in the palace) and a symbol of the strength of established institutions. The building was begun in 1299 and was probably

The first courtyard inside Palazzo Vecchio.

designed by the great architect Arnolfo di Cambio. The original edifice, a massive rusticated cube three storeys high, with great twin-mullioned windows on the two main floors and a battle-mented, covered and projecting passage-way supported on corbels running all around the top of the building. Nine coats of arms symbolizing the various regimes and rulers who have governed the Commune of Florence through the centuries are repeated in the arches formed by the corbels, see for instance the Guelph red lily on white ground and the Ghibelline white lily on a red ground. Trap doors in the floor of the passage were used to drop stones, boiling oil or molten lead on assailants, in the case of uprisings or attacks on the palace. The tower, 94 metres high, placed off-centre, was finished in 1310. The palace was repeatedly enlarged, in 1343, in 1495 (by Cronaca) and in the 16th century by Vasari (who considerably altered the interior) by Giovanni Battista del Tasso and by Buontalenti. The **interior** of the palace is of the greatest interest both architecturally and because of its contents. On the ground floor, the fine **courtyard** by Michelozzo and the **Arms Hall** (entrance on the left side of the palace, used for temporary exhibitions); austere and bare, it is the only 14th century room that has been left unaltered. On the first floor, the magnificent **Hall of the Five Hundred**, with the adjacent **Study of Francesco I**, the **Hall of the Two Hundred** by the brothers Da Maiano (1472-77) with

36

Above: the Hall of the Five Hundred; *below:* detail of the night-assault on Siena, by Vasari. (Palazzo Vecchio).

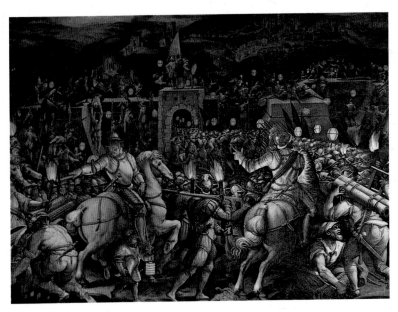

The "Studiolo" or little Study of Francesco I (Palazzo Vecchio).

a fine coffered ceiling in wood (this housed the Council of two hundred citizens who discussed wars and alliances, and is now used by the Borough Council); the **apartments of Leo X**, with a chapel and rooms frescoed with *Scenes from the Lives of the Medicis* by Vasari and helpers (only the rooms of Leo X, Lorenzo the Magnificent and Cosimo I can be visited because the others are occupied by the Mayor and aldermen's offices). On the second floor, the **Apartment of the Elements**, designed by Giovanni Battista del Tasso (c. 1550). These rooms too were decorated by Vasari and helpers, some with fine inlaid cabinets; see also the lovely **Saturn Terrace** with its splendid view; the **Apartments of**

The Room of Clement VII (Palazzo Vecchio).

Eleonora di Toledo, wife of Cosimo I, where special mention should be made of the *Gualdrada room*, with another fine ebony cabinet inlaid with semi-precious stones and the **chapel**, entirely frescoed by Bronzino, who also painted the very fine altar-piece (*Pietà*, 1553); the **chapel of the Signoria**; the very fine **Audience Hall**, with coffered ceiling and marble doorway, both by Benedetto da Maiano, which contains a beautiful wooden bench designed by Vasari; the magnificent **Lily room** with the **Map room** and the **Chancery** next to it; Machiavelli, of whom there is a coloured clay bust and a portrait here, worked in this room for several years as the Secretary of the Republic; and here is the original of the charming fountain in the courtyard, *Cupid with a Dolphin*, by Verrocchio (1476). On the mezzanine (reached from the Hall of the Elements) is a series of 15 rooms containing an important collection of works of art recovered in Germany after World War II. See for instance: the *Crouching Aphrodite*, Roman sculpture, 2nd century A.D.; two fine coloured panels in *opus sectile*, 331 A.D.; Greek and Roman reliefs and sculptures of various epochs. Among the Medieval, Renaissance and later styles exemplified here, note: a beautiful little painting on wood of the *Madonna of Humility* attributed to Masolino and another very small one attributed to Masaccio; a large *Nativity* by Antoniazzo Romano;

The Lily Room (Palazzo Vecchio).

Pygmalion and Galathea by Bronzino; a fragment, barely rough-hewn but very fine, of the *Rondanini Pietà* by Michelangelo; *Venus and Mercury present their son Anteros to Jove*, by Paolo Veronese; *Leda and the Swan*, by Tintoretto; *Portrait of Elizabeth of Valois*, by Coelho; *Judith with the head of Holofernes* and a large *Equestrian portrait of Giovanni Carlo Doria* by Rubens; a beautiful *Portrait of an Unknown Man* by Hans Memling; the *Ecstasy of St. Cecilia* by Bernardo Cavallino; an exquisite *Portrait of Felicita Sartori* by Rosalba Carriera; Venetian landscapes attributed to Francesco Guardi and the circle of Canaletto; and *Maternity* by the 19th century German painter Friedrich von Amerling. Also on the mezzanine are the **Museum of Musical instruments**, containing rare and antique instruments of various periods, and the **Loeser Collection**, an important legacy of sculptures and paintings by Tuscan artists from the 14th to the 16th century. The most important works are: in sculpture, two terracotta groups representing soldiers and knights, by Giovan Francesco Rustici (16th century); a splendid *Madonna and Child*, in painted wood, attributed to the school of Arnolfo di Cambio and a *marble Angel* by Tino da Camaino; in painting: the *Passion of Christ*, a curious work by Piero di Cosimo, end of 15th century: "an abstract and original spirit", Vasari called him in his *Life*; a *Virgin and Child* by Pietro Lorenzetti (first half of 14th century) and the remarkable *Portrait of Laura Battiferri* (wife of the sculptor Ammannati) by Agnolo Bronzino.

Above: the **Wardrobe Room**; *below*: the **Chapel of the Priors**
(Palazzo Vecchio).

The Uffizi, from a print in the Museum of Florence as it was (Museo di Firenze com'era).

UFFIZI GALLERY

The Uffizi is not only the oldest art gallery in the world; it is the most important in Italy and also one of the greatest in Europe and in the whole world, visited by more than a million people every year. The gallery owns about 4800 works, of which about 2000 are on view (1000 paintings, 300 sculptures, 46 tapestries, 14 pieces of furniture and pottery, besides 700 more paintings kept in the Vasari corridor); the rest is in storage or on loan to other museums. This enormous quantity of works includes countless masterpieces, some being among the highest achievements of Western art. The building containing the Gallery was built for

The Uffizi seen from the Arno.

Cosimo I in the mid 16th century in the area between Palazzo Vecchio and the Arno, to house the public offices (hence the name); the 11th century church of San Pietro Scheraggio, and the old Mint, where florins were coined, were partly incorporated. The planning was entrusted to Giorgio Vasari (the author of the *Lives of the artists* as well as court painter and architect), who built it between 1559 and the year of his death (and that of Cosimo), 1574; the building, consists of two long porticoes joined by a third side that abuts on the Arno with a magnificent arch of great scenic effect. The outside of the Uffizi is inspired by the style of Michelangelo's vestibule for the Laurentian Library: grey pietra serena architectural elements against gleaming white plaster. Together with the marvellous Corridor, it is Vasari's architectural masterpiece. Work on the Uffizi was resumed in 1580, by order of Francesco I, and directed by Bernardo Buontalenti, who built the large Medici Theatre (dismantled in 1890) and the famous Tribuna; at the same time the top storey of the loggia was rebuilt, the offices were transferred elsewhere and some of the rooms were used for collections of works of art, arms, and scientific curiosities; and so the Gallery was born. The first nucleus of works already included paintings by Botticelli, Lippi, Paolo Uccello;

about 1600 Ferdinando I had all the works at the Villa Medici in Rome transferred to the Uffizi; in 1631 Ferdinando II contributed an important collection of paintings, (originally in Urbino, the inheritance of his wife Vittoria della Rovere) including works by Piero della Francesca, Titian and Raphael; at the end of the 17th century Cosimo III collected gems, medals and coins and brought the *Venus*, later known as the "Medici" Venus, and other important antique sculptures from Rome; Anna Maria Ludovica, Electress Palatine, the last heir to the Medicis, enlarged the collection with Flemish and German paintings and left it in its entirety to the state of Tuscany in her will (1743). In the nineteenth century, after only part of the works of art robbed during the Napoleonic wars had been restored and after the creation of new specialised museums (Archaelogical Museum, Bargello, Fra Angelico Museum, Science Museums, Silver Museum etc.) the Uffizi became what it is today.

The church of San Piero Scheraggio, inside the Uffizi.

The first corridor of the Uffizi Gallery.

Past the ticket counters, we enter the recently restored church of **San Piero Scheraggio**, traversing the gangway, across the former crypt, on either side of which are Andrea del Castagno's renowned frescoed *Illustrious Men*. Originally painted for the Villa Pandolfini in nearby Legnaia (15th century), they are representations of well-known literary, mythological, and historical figures, from right to left: the Cuman Sibyl, Boccaccio, Petrarch, Dante, Farinata degli Uberti, Pippo Spano, Queen Esther, and Queen Tomiri. The second hall, on the site of the church's apse, contains traces of the original decoration as well as works by 14th century Tuscan painters. Sandro Botticelli's frescoed *Annunciation* graces the hall off to the right. The impressive staircase to the upper floors, designed by Vasari, is decorated with sculptures of various periods, many of which are Roman copies of Greek originals. Off the second floor landing is the entrance to the **Gabinetto dei disegni e delle stampe** (Prints and Drawings Collection). This unique collection, started by Cardinal Leopoldo de'Medici, now comprises over 100,000 pieces by Italian and foreign artists. The vestibule with antique statues on the third floor leads to the first wing of the picture gallery proper.

FIRST WING – The first gallery is the spacious loggia that Buontalenti restructured by order of Francesco I. On either side of the corridor are 4th-

6th century A.D. Roman sarcophagi, as well as Roman busts and statues. The ceiling decoration, in the so-called grotesque style, is by Allori and other 16th century painters. The corridors are sometimes used to display some of the exquisite Flemish and Florentine tapestries in the Uffizi collection.

ROOM I – (At the beginning of the corridor) Roman and Greek sculpture.

ROOM II – This is the hall of the 13th century Italian school. The works displayed here give the observant spectator a splendid chance to perceive how and when Italian painting started to break away from the stiffer, more schematic Byzantine tradition. The forerunners of what would be called the "Renaissance style" are Cimabue, here represented by a superb *Virgin enthroned and Angels*, Duccio di Buoninsegna from Siena with his *Rucellai Madonna* (originally painted for the Rucellai Chapel in the Santa Maria Novella church), and perhaps the most revolutionary of all, Giotto, whose unique *Virgin enthroned* is opposite the entrance. Generally dated 1303-1305, when Giotto was reputedly working on a fresco cycle in Assisi, this painting's naturalism and realistic approach to space and architecture is already a far cry from the schematic Byzantine figures flatly silhouetted against gold ground. In addition, there are works by 13th century artists from the school of Lucca: *St. Francis receiving the Stigmata*, a diptych with the *Virgin and Child surrounded by saints*, and a *Crucifixion* from the school of Bonaventura Berlinghieri. Also *St. Luke the Evangelist* by the Magdalen Master, the *Saviour amidst the Virgin and Saints* by Meliore di Jacopo, and a *Crucifix with scenes of the Passion*, Pisan school 12th century.

ROOM III – This room is filled with splendid examples of the especially refined style that typified 14th century Sienese art. They include major works by the Lorenzetti brothers, two of the foremost Sienese artists of the period: Ambrogio's *Circumcision*, the *Blessed Humility* and *Sts. John, Mark, and Luke*. Perhaps the highlight amongst such treasures is Simone Martini's *Annunciation*, a veritable masterpiece of lyrical grace and refinement. In addition, there is a *Virgin and Child* by Niccolò di Sozzo Tegliacci, a *Nativity* by Simone de' Crocifissi, and a *Presentation at the Temple* by Niccolò Bonaccorsi.

ROOM IV – This room is dedicated to 15th century Florentine painters, especially followers of Giotto. These include Bernardo Daddi's *Virgin and Child* and *Virgin and Child with Saints* (two of the latter subject), Nardo di Cione's *Crucifixion*, Taddeo Gaddi's *Virgin in Glory*, and Giottino's *Pietà*.

ROOMS V-VI – The paintings here are typical examples of late 14th-early 15th century Italian painting. This particular blend of Giottoesque earthiness, Sienese refinement, plus a great profusion of elaborate ornamentations is known as the International Style, the so-called "flowery Gothic." The foremost International style painters are represented here: Gentile da Fabriano (*Adoration of the Magi* and *Four Saints*), Lorenzo Monaco (the huge *Coronation of the Virgin* and another *Adoration of the Magi*), Gherardo Starnina (the *Thebaid*), Agnolo Gaddi (*Crucifixion*), and Giovanni di Paolo (*Virgin and Child with Saints*). The three panels depicting *Scenes from the Life of St. Benedict* are by an unknown Northern Italian artist.

ROOM VII – Contains several famous masterpieces of 15th century painting: *Coronation of the Virgin* and *Virgin and Child* by Fra Angelico, *Virgin and Child surrounded by Saints* by Domenico Veneziano, and the *Virgin and St. Anne* by Masaccio and Masolino (Masaccio's teacher). Also

Left: **Giotto's Madonna Enthroned;** *right*: **Madonna Enthroned by Cimabue** (Uffizi).

Piero della Francesca's double portrait of *Federico da Montefeltro* and *Battista Sforza*. A whole wall is taken up by Paolo Uccello's *Battle of San Romano* which once hung in Lorenzo the Magnificent's bedroom in the Medici-Riccardi Palace.

ROOM VIII – 15th century paintings, mostly by Fra Filippo Lippi (a predella strip of *St. Fregidian deviating the Serchio River;* the *Annunciation of the death of the Virgin*; *St. Augustine in his study*; the *Coronation of the Virgin*, which features fine portraits of several of Lippi's contemporaries; an altarpiece with the *Annunciation and saints*; the charming *Virgin and Child and two Angels*; an *Adoration of the Babe with St. Hilarion*; and another *Adoration with Sts. John and Romualdus*). Other painters represented are Alessio Baldovinetti (*Annunciation* and *Virgin and Child surrounded by Saints*), Lorenzo Vecchietta (*Virgin enthroned*), and Nicholas Froments (triptych depicting the *Resurrection of Lazarus*).

ROOM IX – The seated *Virtues* are by Antonio Pollaiolo, except for *Fortitude* by Botticelli. Antonio and Piero Pollaiolo, together, painted the fine portrait of *Galeazzo Sforza*. The *Portrait of a Youth with a red beret* is by Filippino Lippi, son of Filippo and pupil of Botticelli.

ROOMS X-XIV – This area is mostly devoted to works by the great master of line and color, Sandro Botticelli, whose brilliant grace typified 15th century Florentine painting; the most famous: the *Birth of Venus* and the *Allegory of Spring*, both impregnated with symbolic meanings; the *Madon-*

Adoration of the Magi, by Gentile da Fabriano (Uffizi).

na del Magnificat; the *Calumny*; the *Annunciation*; the *Adoration of the Magi* and the *Portrait of a Young Man with a medallion*. The room also contains works by Roger Van der Weyden, Ghirlandaio, Filippino Lippi, and Hugo Van der Goes' superb *Portinari Altarpiece*.

ROOM XV – Contains two famous works by Leonardo da Vinci: *The Annunciation* and the *Adoration of the Magi*, as well as a remarkable *Deposition* by Perugino and a recently restored *Crucifixion* by Signorelli.

ROOM XVI – Or the Map Room, frescoed with maps of Tuscany by Buonsignori.

ROOM XVII – This room is entered through the "Tribuna.". Two important Hellenistic sculptures are here: *Amor and Psyche* and the famous *Sleeping Hermaphrodite* (2nd century B.C.).

Above: **Allegory of Spring**; *below*: **the Birth of Venus, two of Alessandro Botticelli's most famous paintings** (Uffizi).

The Annunciation, by Leonardo da Vinci (Uffizi).

ROOM XVIII – The "**Tribuna**" was designed by Buontalenti c. 1589 as a showcase for the Medici's most treasured pieces. Standing in the middle is the renowned *Medici Venus*, a Greek masterpiece of the 3rd century B.C. The walls are hung with 16th century portraits by several of the best-known Mannerist painters (16th century). Two female portraits by Bronzino are especially handsome — *Eleonora di Toledo* and *Lucrezia Panciatichi*. There are also fine paintings by Rosso Fiorentino, Vasari, and Pontormo, not to mention the many pieces of Greek and Roman sculpture, inlaid furniture, and a mother-of-pearl dome.

ROOM XIX – The paintings in this room come from the Central Italian schools, including outstanding works by Perugino (portraits and a *Virgin between Sts. John the Baptist and Sebastian*) and by Luca Signorelli (the *Holy Family Tondo*, and a *Virgin and Child*, two of Signorelli's finest paintings). There is also a lovely *Annunciation* by Melozzo da Forlì and works by two painters greatly influenced by Perugino, Lorenzo Costa and Gerolamo Genga.

ROOM XX – Devoted to the German school, with several well-known paintings by one of the greatest German painters, Dürer: the *Calvary* (next to it is Brueghel's copy), portraits of *St. James the Greater* and *St. Philip the Apostle*, the *Adoration of the Magi*, *Portrait of the Artist's Father*, and a *Virgin and Child*. The *Portraits of Luther and His Wife*, *Luther and Melanchthon*, and *Adam and Eve* are by Lucas Cranach.

ROOM XXI – Dedicated to 15th century Venetian painting with an emphasis on Giorgione and Giovanni Bellini. The latter is represented by *Portrait of a gentleman*, *Sacred Allegory* whose esoteric symbolism is made even more mysterious by the daylight setting, and the *Lamentation of Christ*. Giorgione's works are *Moses before Pharaoh* and the *Judgement of Solomon*. Also, paintings by other Northern Italian artists: the *Warriors and the Old Men*, by Carpaccio, *St. Louis of Toulouse* by Bartolomeo Vivarini, *Christ in the Temple* by Giovanni Mansueti, the delicate *Virgin and Child* by Cima da Conegliano, and *St. Dominic* by Cosmè Tura.

ROOM XXII – Paintings by Northern Renaissance painters, Hans Holbein, the including portrait painter (*Self-portrait and Portrait of Sir Richard Southwell*), Gerard David (the dramatic *Adoration of the Magi*), Lukas van

The "Tribuna" in the Uffizi.

Leyden (*Christ crowned with thorns*) and Albert Altdorfer (*Life of St. Florian*).

ROOM XXIII – Contains paintings by Antonio Allegri, better known as Correggio (1489-1534), who was greatly influenced by Leonardo. Correggio's hallmark, soft color and no contours, is evident in the works displayed here (the *Virgin in Glory*, the *Rest on the Flight to Egypt*, and the *Adoration*). The *Adoration of the Shepherds and the Madonna delle Cave*, by Andrea Mantegna are also here.

ROOM XXIV – Generally closed to the public, this room contains Italian and foreign miniatures from the 15th to 18th centuries.

SECOND WING – This section connects the two main corridors of the Uffizi. The works displayed are Roman sculptures. See: the *Boy removing a thorn from his foot, Venus*, two *Roman matrons*, and the *Girl preparing for the dance*. From the great western window in the second (shorter) gallery, one enjoys a splendid view of the Ponte Vecchio with the **Vasari corridor** running over it. Conceived as an aerial passage linking Palazzo Vecchio by means of a short bridge to the Uffizi, which are linked to the Grandducal residence of Palazzo Pitti by means of the Corridor proper. This singular feat of architecture and town planning was executed in the short space of five months, in 1565, by Giorgio Vasari, commissioned by Cosimo I. The Vasari Corridor starts from the Uffizi on the third floor between Room XXV and Room XXXIV, runs along the Arno over an arcade, crosses the river over Ponte Vecchio, passes between houses and palaces on the other side of the river, traverses the façade of the church of

Santa Felicita, continues along the side of Boboli Garden and, after a distance of nearly a kilometre, enters the Pitti Palace. It was damaged in World War II and only reopened in 1973; one has to book visits in groups. About seven hundred paintings are on view, including 17th and 18th century Italian works, portraits of the Medicis and the Hapsburgs, and above all the famous **collection of self-portraits**, the most complete in the world, extending from the 14th century to the present time, including nearly all the greater Italian artists and numerous foreign ones.

THIRD WING – This corridor too is decorated with some fine Roman sculptures, mainly dating from the 2nd through the 4th century A.D. At the beginning are two statues of *Marsyas before his Flaying* (the one on the right was retouched by Donatello). Farther on are a *Discus-thrower, Leda and the Swan,* and other Greek mythological figures.

ROOM XXV – Displayed here among other masterpieces of 16th century painting is one of Michelangelo's rare panel paintings, the so-called *Doni Tondo,* commissioned by Angelo Doni. The subject is the Holy Family. See also a *Portrait of Perugino,* attributed to Raphael, as well as works by Rosso Fiorentino and Mariotto Albertinelli, two well known Tuscan Mannerists.

ROOM XXVI – The Raphael room: the famous *Madonna del Cardellino, Leo X with Cardinals Giulio de' Medici and Luigi de' Rossi, Self-portrait* (on an easel), and *Portrait of Francesco Maria della Rovere* are all here. In addition, Andrea del Sarto *Madonna delle Arpie* (Virgin of the Harpies), not to mention fine works by Mannerists such as Pontormo (the *Martyrdorm of St. Maurice*) and several portraits.

ROOM XXVII – This room is devoted to two of the foremost 16th century Mannerist painters, Bronzino and Pontormo. The *Holy Family, Lamentation of Christ,* and the refined *Portrait of a lady* are by Bronzino, whereas the *Supper at Emmaus,* the *Birth of St. John the Baptist, Portrait of a musician, Portrait of Maria Salviati,* and the *Virgin and Saints* were painted by Pontormo. There are also works by Franciabigio and Rosso Fiorentino.

ROOM XXVIII – This room is devoted to Titian (1477-1576) whose rich palette and emphatic use of light and shade became the hallmark of the Venetian school. Perhaps the best-known are the *Venus of Urbino,* the *Flora,* the *Portraits of Eleonora Gonzaga,* and *Francesca Maria della Rovere,* duke and duchess of Urbino, and *Venus and Cupid.* A follower of Titian's, Palma il Vecchio, painted the *Resurrection of Lazarus,* the *Sacra Conversazione,* and *Judith.*

ROOM XXIX – Several of Parmigianino's (1505-1540) finest works are hanging here: the *Virgin and Child with Saints,* a *Portrait of an Unknown Gentleman,* and the magnificent *Madonna dal Collo Lungo* (the Virgin with the long neck). Other artists represented are Ludovico Mazzolino, Luca Cambiaso, Scarsellino, and Girolamo da Carpi.

ROOM XXX – The painters represented here belong to the Central Italian Emilia-Romagna school. Mazzolino is represented by the *Circumcision of Christ* and the *Virgin and St. Anne.*

ROOM XXXI – Several works by Dosso Dossi, a Ferrarese artist greatly influenced by the Venetian school: *Portrait of a soldier,* the *Virgin in Glory,* and *Witchcraft.* Paintings by 16th century Venetians such as Lorenzo Lotto and Sebastiano del Piombo are also displayed.

Michelangelo's world-famous Doni Tondo (Uffizi).

ROOM XXXII – This room contains works by a prominent Venetian artist, Sebastiano del Piombo (1485-1547), known for his skillful fashion of modelling luminous colour into forms. A fine example is the *Death of Adonis* hanging here, by many considered his masterpiece. In addition, works by Lorenzo Lotto (*Sacra Conversazione, Susanna and the Elders*) and Paris Bordone (two portraits) are exhibited.

ROOM XXXIII – Also known as the "16th Century Hall" this passageway is hung with late 16th century Italian and foreign works including François Clouet's *Portrait of Francis I*, Alessandro Allori's *Portrait of Torquato Tasso*, Bronzino's *Allegory of Happiness*, and Jacopo Ligozzi's *Three Ages of Man*.

ROOM XXXIV – This room is devoted to Paolo Caliari better known as Veronese (1528-1588), one of the foremost 16th century Venetian school painters. Displayed are his *St. Agatha crowned by Angels*, the *Martyrdom of St. Justine*, the *Annunciation*, and the *Holy Family*. Other artists whose works hang here include Giulio Campi and Giovanni Battista Moroni, two prominent 16th century portrait painters.

Left: **Selfportrait, by Leonardo da Vinci;** *right:* **Selfportrait, by Lorenzo Bernini** (Vasari Corridor).

ROOM XXXV – Here one can admire important works by Tintoretto (1518-1595) whose style is a combination of startling light and shade contrasts emphasizing intensely animated composition. The result is a uniquely dramatic effect that is typified in the *Good Samaritan*, the *Apparition of St. Augustine*, *Leda*, *Portrait of Jacopo Sansovino*, and *Portrait of a red-haired man*. The *Story of Joseph*, *Annunciation to the Shepherds*, and *Portrait of the Artist* are by another renowned 16th century Venetian artist, Jacopo Bassani. In addition, there are works by Federico Barocci and El Greco.

From Room XXXV you go directly to Room XLI as Rooms XXXVI to XL were eliminated when the newly-restored *Buontalenti Staircase* was re-opened.

ROOM XLI – Works by the Flemish masters Rubens and Van Dyck are here. Rubens' (1577-1640) impressive canvases of *Henry IV's triumphal entrance into Paris* and *Henry IV at the Battle of Ivry*, as well as two of his portraits, one of his wife *Isabel* and one of *Emperor Charles V* offer splendid insight into the Flemish painter's exuberant style. Anthony Van Dyck's portraits are incomparably skillful, as is Susterman's *Portrait of Galileo*.

ROOM XLIII – The Caravaggio room, with the *Medusa*, *Bacchus* and the *Sacrifice of Isaac* by this great master of light and shade contrasts (1573-1610).

ROOM XLIV – Contains three magnificent works by Rembrandt van Rijn (1606-1669): two *Self-portraits* and a *Portrait of an old man*.

ROOM XLV – Among the paintings here are two charming *Views of Venice*, by Canaletto (1698-1768), a pair of *Capriccios* by Francesco Guardi (1712-1793) and two superb Goya *Portraits* (1746-1828).
Midway along the third gallery is the exit, preceded by a vestibule containing the marble Hellenistic *Wild Boar*, copied by Pietro Tacca in bronze for the Loggia of the New Market.

THIRD ITINERARY

*Piazza della Repubblica - Straw Market -
Ponte Vecchio -
Pitti Palace - Boboli Gardens - Santo Spirito -
Santa Maria del Carmine*

Piazza della Repubblica with the ancient Column of the Market.

PIAZZA DELLA REPUBBLICA

In Roman times the city Forum stood where this piazza is today; there was a Temple of Jove and a column at the crossing of the two principal streets, *cardo* and *decumanus*, (respectively, the axis, Via degli Speziali - Via Strozzi, and Via Calimala - Via Roma). The Old Market, with its hovels, towers, loggias, stores and shops, all clustering round a column — known as the Column in the Market — on which was a statue of Plenty, replaced several times, superseded the Forum in medieval times. In the 19th century, after an epidemic of cholera, the Commune decided to "wipe out centuries of squalor", as the plaque over the archway reads, and pulled down the whole complex, replacing it with the pompous architecture of today's square.

The Palace of the Guelph Party Captains.

From Piazza della Repubblica, along Via Pellicceria (the road with the porticos) one gets to the **Palagio dei Capitani di parte Guelfa** (the Palace of the Guelph Captains). The building stands in the small piazza of the same name, one of the most picturesque places in medieval Florence. Built in the 14th century, it has a small, elegant façade with an outside staircase; it was enlarged in the 15th century (by Brunelleschi) and again by Vasari at the end of the 16th century. The powerful magistrature that it housed was established in 1267, when the Guelphs defeated the Ghibellines. To the left of the Palace, Via Valdilamona leads to the Straw Market, a picturesque, busy little market of articles of Florentine craftsmanship under the **Loggia del Mercato Nuovo** by Giovan Battista del Tasso (1547-51). The square based loggia was ordered by Cosimo I for some of the most important corporations such as the bankers and the dealers in gold, wool and silk. Beside it is the entertaining Boar Fountain (Porcellino) by Pietro Tacca (1612). To the left of Via Por Santa Maria, the road connecting the Straw Market to the Ponte Vecchio, is the ancient church of **Santo Stefano al Ponte** in the little square named after the church, which has a simple Romanesque façade and a doorway decorated with marble in two colours (end of 13th century). The interior, with a single nave, was restored by Tacca in the 16th century; the structure of the unusual, highly elegant presbytery, preceded by a flight of steps by Buontalenti (1574) is flanked by a large altar on either side; there is a 16th century choir with a coffered ceiling: third altar on the left, bronze frontal with the *Martyrdom of St. Stephen*, by Tacca.

Above: the Loggia of the New Market; *below*: detail of the Fountain of the Boar (Porcellino).

Aerial view of the Ponte Vecchio (Old Bridge).

PONTE VECCHIO

As the name implies (Old Bridge), it is the oldest bridge in Florence: it has, in fact, existed since the time of the Roman colony, when the piers were of stone and the roadway of wood; destroyed by flooding in 1117 it was completely rebuilt in stone but collapsed again in the terrible flood of November 4th 1333; it was rebuilt for the last time in 1345 with three spans, very wide, planned with room for shops on either side. First of all the butchers settled there (but later also grocers, smiths, shoemakers etc.); these built the typical shops projecting over the river, resting on supports and brackets. In 1591 Ferdinando I evicted them all only allowing the shops to the goldsmiths; and since then the bridge has been like two long jewellery-shop windows, only interrupted by the two clearings in the middle; the one looking downstream has a bust of Benvenuto Cellini, "master of the goldsmiths" by Raffaello Romanelli (1900).

Leaving Ponte Vecchio and going along Via Guicciardini towards Piazza Pitti, we encounter the Church of **Santa Felicita** on our left, in its little square, built on the site of an early Christian basilica of the 4th century; several times rebuilt, the last time by Ruggieri in the 17th century. The Vasari Corridor runs across the top of the façade of the church. The Medici family used to sit in the pew in the Corridor, looking into the church through the gilded grate, having walked to attend the religious services from Palazzo Pitti without setting a foot out of doors. Inside, on

Above: **the centre of the Ponte Vecchio with the bust of B. Cellini;** *below:* **the Vasari Corridor along the Arno.**

the altar of the Capponi Chapel (first on the right) is a magnificent *Descent from the Cross* by Pontormo (c. 1528); on the right wall an *Annunciation*, also by Pontormo; in the sacristy, a *polyptych* by Taddeo Gaddi.
At the end of Via Guicciardini, one emerges into Piazza Pitti, with the gigantic golden bulk of Palazzo Pitti at the top of the slope to our left.

View of the façade of Pitti Palace.

PITTI PALACE

By the middle of the 15th century, power was practically in the hands of the Medici family; Cosimo the Elder governed Florence from his new palace in Via Larga; Luca Pitti, at one time his friend, now led the faction that was most hostile to him and to his son Piero. Luca, wanted a palace finer than the one that Michelozzo was building for the Medicis. He chose the site, on the hill of Boboli, and commissioned Brunelleschi to design a building with windows as large as the doorways of the Medici palace and so large, that the Medici palace would fit into his courtyard. Brunelleschi accepted with alacrity (his own plan for Via Larga had been rejected at the time) and produced the plans about 1445. Work began in 1457 (after the master's death) under the direction of Luca Fancelli, Brunelleschi's pupil. The façade overlooking the piazza consisted only of the seven central windows; it was on three storeys separated by slender balconies and covered with rusticated stone. At the death of Luca Pitti in 1473 the palace was still incomplete; then the Pitti family fell into disfavour, and Eleonora di Toledo, the wife of Cosimo I, bought the building and the land behind it in 1549. In the 16th and 17th century this became the palace of the Medici, who enlarged it, created a garden on the Boboli hill, lengthened the building to nine windows each side, employing Giulio and Alfonso Parigi, and decorated the interior sumptuously. In the 18th century Ruggieri and Poccianti built the

The Ammannati Courtyard in Pitti Palace.

two porticoed side wings that enclose the piazza. The remarkable fact is that each successive enlargement substantially respected the original design by Brunelleschi, both in form and material. During the period in which Florence was the capital of Italy (1865-71) the palace was the residence of Vittorio Emanuele II. Since 1919 it has been the property of the Italian State, together with its magnificent collections formed in centuries of devotion to art. There are seven museums here: the **Palatine Gallery**, the **Monumental Apartments**, the **Silver Museum**, the **Gallery of Modern Art**, the **Gallery of Costumes**, the **Coach Museum** and the **Porcelain Museum**.

The main doorway leads into the majestic Ammannati courtyard (1558-1570), which is dominated by the *Artichoke Fountain* on the terrace above, on the garden side. There are two smaller fountains dedicated to Hercules, beneath the terrace, flanking the Moses Grotto, decorated with allegorical marble and porphyry statues. The staircase on the right leads up to the first floor where one enters the Palatine Gallery.

THE PALATINE GALLERY – SALA DI VENERE (Venus Room) – The ceiling was frescoed by Pietro da Cortona and Ciro Ferri and adorned with exquisite stuccowork by Roman artists (1641-1642). Several extraordinary paintings are hanging here, including Titian's renowned *"La Bella"*, probably a portrait of Duchess Eleonora Gonzaga from Urbino, a *Sacra Conversazione* by Bonifacio de' Pitati, two *Seascapes* by Salvator Rosa, and *Portrait of Pietro Aretino*, one of Titian's late works. In addition, there is another Titian, a *Portrait of Julius II* which is a copy of a Raphael, to whom the painting was once attributed as a youthful work. Another Titian here,

61

The Venus Room (Palatine Gallery).

the *Concert*, once attributed to his master, Giorgione, and now thought to be an early work, painted by Titian, while still in Giorgione's workshop. There are two Rubens: the *Peasants' return from the fields* and *Ulysses on the Isle of the Phaecians*. Francesco Bassano painted the *Martyrdom of St. Catherine* and Guercino *Apollo and Marsyas*.

SALA DI APOLLO (Apollo Room) – The ceiling fresco is by Pietro da Cortona and Ciro Ferri (1647-1660). The series of great Titians continues here with the *Magdalen* and the *Portrait of the grey-eyed youth*. In addition, there is a superb Tintoretto, *Portrait of Vincenzo Zeno*, as well as *Nymph chased by a satyr* and *St. John the Baptist* by Dosso Dossi, the *Holy Family* and a magnificent *Deposition*, by Andrea del Sarto, a splendid altarpiece by the Mannerist painter Rosso Fiorentino of the *Virgin and Saints*, a fine self-portrait by Andrea del Sarto, and lastly a double portrait by Anthony Van Dyck, *Charles I of England and Henrietta Maria, his French Bourbon queen*.

SALA DI MARTE (Mars Room) – The ceiling fresco was again painted by Pietro da Cortona and Ciro Ferri (1646). In addition to two charming versions of the *Virgin and Child* by the Spanish artist, Murillo, there are two major Rubens: a portrait group entitled the *Four Philosophers* (the first

Above: **Seascape, by Salvator Rosa;** *below*: **the Gentleman with the grey eyes and the Beauty, two splendid portraits by Titian.**

The Consequences of War, by P.P. Rubens (Palatine Gallery).

standing figure on the left is a self-portrait) and the renowned *Consequences of War*, a huge canvas painted by Rubens in Antwerp in 1638. Commissioned by Ferdinando II, the subject was inspired by the bloody Thirty Years' War. Two fine Titian portraits: *Ipppolito de' Medici* and *Andrea Vesalio*, Van Dyck's *Portrait of Cardinal Bentivoglio* considered one of his finest, Tintoretto's *Portrait of Luigi Cornaro*, and Veronese's *Portrait of Daniele Barbaro*. Also works by Guido Reni and Guercino.

SALA DI GIOVE (Jupiter Room) – The mythological scenes on the ceiling are by Pietro da Cortona and Ferri (1643-1645). In the middle of the room is a marble statue of *Victory* by Vincenzo Consani (1867). One of Raphael's best-known paintings. *La Velata* (Lady with a veil) is here. The model who sat for the portrait was probably Raphael's mistress, *la Fornarina* (the baker girl), who often served as his model. Other fine paintings in the room: Borgognone's *Battle scene*, Andrea del Sarto's, *Portrait of the artist and his wife* and his charming *Annunciation*, Bronzino's *Portrait of Guidobaldo della Rovere*, Rubens' *Nymphs chased by satyrs*, and Fra Bartolomeo's striking *Deposition*.

SALA DI SATURNO (Saturn Room) – The ceiling fresco by Ferri (1663-1665) is based upon a design by Pietro da Cortona. This room contains a number of Raphael's major works, including the much loved *Madonna of the Chair*, where the figures' full, rounded forms belong to the artist's Roman period; *the Portrait of Cardinal Dovizi da Bibbiena*; the unfinished *Madonna del Baldacchino* (Virgin of the Canopy); and the *Wedding portraits of Agnolo*

The Four Philosophers, by P.P. Rubens (Palatine Gallery).

and Maddalena Doni. Also the famous *Madonna del Granduca* of 1505. A subtle blend of Leonardesque and Umbrian influence (Raphael' early style is a grew up in Umbria where he studied under Perugino). Also here: Perugino's *Deposition* painted in Florence in 1495 and the *Magdalen*, with its intense light and shade contrasts. Also: Ridolfo del Ghirlandaio's *Portrait of a goldsmith* and Guercino's *St. Sebastian*.

SALA DELL'ILIADE (Iliad Room) – The ceiling decoration by Luigi Sabatelli portrays episodes from Homer's Iliad. The statue in the middle by Lorenzo Bartolini (1824) represents *Charity*. The highlights of the room are Velasquez's *Portrait of Philip IV of Spain*, a series of end of the 16th — beginning of the 17th century portraits, by Justus Sustermans, the official portrait painter to the Medici court at the time, and a *Portrait of King Philip II of Spain* by Titian, also two *Assumptions* by Andrea del Sarto and Raphael's Portrait of a lady known as *La Gravida* (the pregnant woman) painted in Florence when Raphael was still influenced by Leonardo.

SALA DELL'EDUCAZIONE DI GIOVE (Room of the Education of Jupiter) – (To the right of the Sala dell'Iliade). The room was named after the mythological scene of the ceiling fresco by Luigi Catani (1819). The paintings displayed are a striking *Portrait of a man* by Van Dyck, Caravaggio's famous *Sleeping Cupid*, a *Pietà* by Francesco Salviati, and the *Chaste Susanna* by Guercino. The head of Holofernes in Cristoforo Allori's *Judith* is supposedly a self-portrait of the artist.

Left: **the Veiled Lady;** *right:* **the Madonna of the Grandduke, two of Raphael's masterpieces in the Palatine Gallery.**

SALA DELLA STUFA (Room of the Stove) – The walls and ceiling of this room are entirely frescoed by Matteo Rosselli and Pietro da Cortona with the allegorical scenes of the Golden, Silver, Bronze and Iron Ages.

SALETTA DA BAGNO (Bath) – The neo-Classical decorative scheme of stuccowork and bas-reliefs is by Giuseppe Cacialli.

SALA DI ULISSE (Ulysses Room) – The ceiling fresco by Gaspare Martellini depicting *Ulysses' return to Ithaca* was meant to symbolize Ferdinando III's return to Florence after Napoleon's defeat. There are several paintings by the 17th century painter Carlo Dolci (the *Virgin and Child* is especially charming). Cigoli's *Ecce Homo*, Tintoretto's *Portrait of Andrea Frazier*, Filippino Lippi's *Death of Lucretia*, Raphael's *Madonna dell'Impannata (impannata* indicates the oiled cloth on the window) and a *Portrait of Alfonso di Ferrara* attributed to Titian.

SALA DI PROMETEO (Prometheus Room) – The frescoed ceiling and walls, by Giuseppe Collignon (1842), depict scenes from the myth of Prometheus. The paintings in the room include Pontormo's *11,000 martyrs*, Albertinelli's *Holy Family* and Luca Signorelli's treatment of the same subject, Filippo Lippi's charming tondo of the *Virgin and Child* and Francesco Botticini's *Virgin and Child with Angels*.

POCCETTI GALLERY – The ceiling was frescoed by Bernardo Poccetti (16th cent.). There two portraits by Rubens, *Ila and the nymphs* by Francesco Furini, the *Martyrdom of St. Bartholomew* by Ribera, four *landscapes* by Poussin, and the *Missing drachma* by Domenico Feti.

The Room of the Stove (Palatine Gallery).

SALA DELLA MUSICA (Music Room) – It is also known as the Drum Room from the drum-shaped furniture. The table in the middle is made of Russian malachite and has gilded bronze supports.

SALA CASTAGNOLI – The room was named after the painter who decorated it in the 19th century. The round *table* in the middle is inlaid with precious stones. Made in Florence in 1851, and known as the "Table of the Muses" it shows Apollo in his chariot surrounded by symbols of Muses. The bronze support with *Seasons and cupids* is by Giovanni Duprè.

SALA DELLE ALLEGORIE (Allegory Room) – The room is also known as "Sala del Volterrano" (Volterrano is the name of the painter who frescoed the allegorical scenes). The paintings include the *Pranks of Pievano Arlotto, Profane Venus*, and *Sleeping Cupid* also by Volterrano, the *Virgin and Child* by Artemisia Gentileschi, as well as *Venus and Amor* and the *Wedding Night* by Giovanni da San Giovanni.

SALA DELLE ARTI (Art Room) – Frescoed by Podestà (19th century). Paintings by Doldi, Ligozzi, and Rustici, and an *Adoration of the Magi* by Cristoforo Allori.

SALA DI ERCOLE (Hercules Room) – Pietro Benvenuti frescoed *Stories of Hercules* in the neo-Classical style. Also a splendid *Sèvres vase*, a present from Napoleon to Ferdinand III.

SALA DELL'ARCA (Ark Room) – Frescoed in 1816 by Luigi Ademollo to represent the pavilion David built for the Ark.

CAPPELLA DELLE GRANDUCHESSE (the Chapel of the Grand-duchesses, also known as the Reliquary Chapel) – Decorated with gilded stuccowork and frescoes, in the early 17th century for Maria Magdalen of Austria as a private chapel for the grandduchesses.

THE MONUMENTAL OR EX-ROYAL APARTMENTS – These magnificent apartments were the living quarters of the Medici, the Hapsburg granddukes, and in the 19th century, of the Savoy family, the Italian sovereigns.

The first room, or Dining Hall is also called the SALA DELLE NICCHIE (Niches Room).

SALA VERDE (Green room) is hung with Gobelins tapestries. The allegorical frescoes honoring the Medici are by Luca Giordano.

SALA DEL TRONO (Throne room) was where the kings of Italy took oath. The room contains portraits by Sustermans and Francesco Porbus, as well as magnificient maiolica vases.

SALA CELESTE (Blue Room) is decorated with Gobelins tapestries, portraits by Sustermans, and rare Chinese vases.

The CHAPEL with portraits of Medici Cardinals by Sustermans.

The SALA DEI PAPPAGALLI (Parrot Room) was named for the parrot motifs in the tapestries. There are paintings by Titian (*Portrait of the Duchess of Urbino*) and Hans von Aachen (*Portrait of Francesco I*). This room and the following two were Queen Margherita of Italy's Suite. The SALA GIALLA (Yellow Room), is hung with Gobelin tapestries, as well as portraits, one, attributed to J.F. Douven depicts the *Electress Palatine*.

Back in the Sala dei Pappagalli, we enter King Umberto I's suite. The bedroom, study, and living room are decorated with tapestries and portraits.The SALA DI BONA was frescoed by Poccetti with scenes showing the *Conquest of the city of Bona in Africa*, the *Conquest of Prevesa, a View of Leghorn harbor*, and an *Apotheosis of Cosimo I*.

SALA BIANCA (White Room), the ballroom's ceiling and walls are covered with Neo-classical stuccos. Beautiful chandeliers. Used by the Hapsburgs and the Savoy Sovereigns for official receptions.

After viewing the Palatine Gallery and the Royal Apartments, we go up to the second floor of the palace and enter the Gallery of Modern Art.

The Throne Room (The "Royal" Apartments).

THE GALLERY OF MODERN ART – Founded by the Tuscan provisional government in 1860, this museum contains a fascinating Italian 19th century collection. In addition to the neo-Classical and academic schools profusely represented, there are also numerous paintings belonging to a Tuscan movement called "I Macchiaioli" (from macchia = splash or mark) which was akin and contemporary but not influenced by the French Impressionist Movement. The "Macchiaioli" artists strived to free themselves from the restrictions and conventions of academic art, seeking for inspiration in nature and reality. Works by the head of the movement, Giovanni Fattori, and of all its major exponents: Silvestro Lega, Telemaco Signorini, Giuseppe Abbati, Raffaele Sernesi, may be viewed. There are also works by artists alive today.

THE SILVER MUSEUM – Instituted in 1919 and arranged on the ground floor of Pitti Palace, in the rooms that were used as the summer apartments of the Grand Dukes. Among the most interesting of these, from the point of view of decoration, are the Room of Giovanni da San Giovanni and the three successive ones, frescoed by Colonna and Mitelli between 1638 and 1644. The collection includes goldsmiths' work, enamels, cameos, crystal and carved or inlaid semi-precious stone objects, collected by the Medicis and the Hapsburgs. Among the most important pieces are: semi-precious stone vases belonging to the Magnificent Lorenzo; 17th century German ivories; a vase in lapis lazuli by Buontalenti (1583): the

**The Giovanni di San Giovanni Room and the Mermaid Pendant
from the Collection of Medici Jewellery in the Silver Museum.**

jewels of the bishop-princes of Salzburg; drinking cup belonging to Diane de Poitiers (16th century); relief of *Cosimo II in prayer* (17th century).

THE COACH MUSEUM (The entrance is under the arcade of the right wing of the palace). This fascinating little museum contains the carriages in use from the 16th through 19th centuries, as well as fittings and costumes dating from various periods. In the entrance hall are precious fittings that once belonged to the Medici and to the Savoy Sovereigns. In addition, prints showing costumes of the Medici court in the 18th century. The second room contains the exhibition of coaches, among which is the sedan belonging to the Electress Palatine Maria Luisa (18th century), the coaches belonging to the Duke of Modena, Francesco II (17th century), the Grandduke of Tuscany, Leopoldo II (1815); the King of Naples, Ferdinando (1839); Caterina de' Medici (16th century), as well as the special chair Grandduke Cosimo II used for going up and down stairs, after his legs were paralyzed.

Back in the square, one goes through the left wing gateway (the Arno river side), leading into the Boboli Gardens.

BOBOLI GARDENS

The gardens were laid out on the Boboli hill shortly after Pitti Palace became the property of Cosimo I and Eleonora of Toledo, towards the second half of the 16th century. Michelangelo's pupil, the architect and sculptor Niccolò Pericoli, called "Tribolo", was given the task of designing a garden in accordance with the new Renaissance mode, which exacted more stately proportions than

Detail of the Neptune Fountain (Boboli Gardens).

the Medieval private "viridarium" (or greenery) had accustomed people to. A Renaissance garden was the symbol of a prince's power, the scene of parties and plays, a place of relaxation for the court, where one could wander through groves populated by allegorical statues, grottoes, fountains. Boboli underwent many alterations owing to variations in taste, but the design remained substantially the same. Near the entrance is the curious *Bacchus Fountain* in which Valerio Cioli portrayed a dwarf of the court of Cosimo I astride a tortoise; further on is the *Grotto by Buontalenti*, built between 1583 and 1588 for the eccentric Francesco I; the first chamber is like a real cave in decorated with sculptured forms that, on closer examination, look like animals; in the corners are four copies of Michelangelo's *Prisoners* (Accademia Gallery) which used to be here; in the cave behind, the group of *Paris and Helena*,

The Bacchus Fountain (Boboli Gardens).

by Vincenzo de' Rossi; last comes a small grotto with a *Venus* by Giambologna. Going on one comes to the *Amphitheatre*, first made in grass in the 16th century and remade in the 18th, for the performance of plays; the obelisk in the centre was brought to Rome from Luxor in the Imperial epoch. Going up to the left one comes to the Neptune fishpond and the *Giardino del Cavaliere*, where the **Porcelain Museum** is; or going straight on, along a wide avenue, one reaches the beautiful Piazzale dell'Isolotto, with its large pool and island planted with lemon trees and the *Ocean Fountain* by Giambologna. The garden is full of other antique and Renaissance statues.

From piazza Pitti, one crosses piazza San Felice and turns right into Via Mazzetta to which leads to **Piazza Santo Spirito**, one of the most attractive squares in Florence. Number 10 is Palazzo Guadagni, an outstanding Florentine Renaissance palace, attributed to Cronaca (1503-1506). The building is crowned by a graceful loggia and sports a lovely wrought-iron lantern on the corner.

The church of Santo Spirito overlooking its square.

SANTO SPIRITO

The church of Santo Spirito stands south of the Arno river. The original plan, by Filippo Brunelleschi (1444), was for a church facing in the opposite direction, with the façade towards the Arno overlooking a large piazza; but it could not be carried out owing to the opposition of the landowners involved. Brunelleschi's design was largely respected, as regards the interior, after the master's death by Antonio Manetti and other pupils; while the simple façade is 17th century. The slender **bell-tower** was built by Baccio d'Agnolo at the beginning of the 16th century. The spacious and solemn **interior** recalls the symmetry and rhythmical perfection achieved by Brunelleschi in San Lorenzo, except for the variation of a dome above the presbytery and the continuation of the side aisles in the transept and the apse. The Baroque high altar, by Giovanni Caccini (1608) stands in the centre of the

73

presbytery. In the right transept is a fine *Virgin and Child with Saints and Patrons* by Filippo Lippi (c. 1490) with an interesting view of Florence in the background. In the apse is a polyptych by Maso di Banco representing the *Virgin and Child with Saints*; on a nearby altar is a painting of the *Holy Martyrs* by Alessandro Allori (1574); in the predella is a view of the first façade of Pitti Palace. In the left transept is the Corbinelli Chapel, an elegant piece of architecture and sculpture by Andrea Sansovino (1492); next to it is the *Holy Trinity with Sts. Catherine and Magdalen*, attributed to Francesco Granacci. Off the left aisle is an elegant vestibule by Cronaca (1494) with a fine barrel vault; this leads into the beautiful octagonal **Sacristy**, with dome, by Giuliano da Sangallo (1492). Leaving the church, on the right is the entrance to the **Cenacolo**, or refectory of the Augustinian monastery that used to exist here; the wall at the end of the room is covered by a large fresco by Andrea Orcagna (c. 1360) representing two scenes, one above the other: a wonderful *Crucifixion* and a *Last Supper* (now in very poor condition).

Crossing the square, we turn right into Via Sant'Agostino, cross Via de' Serragli, and continue down Via Santa Monica until we come to **Piazza del Carmine**.

SANTA MARIA DEL CARMINE

With Santo Spirito, this is the most important church on the south side of the Arno. It was founded in 1268 by the Carmelite Friars. In 1771 it was burnt down, except for the Corsini and Brancacci chapels and the sacristy; the parts destroyed were completely rebuilt a few years later. The unfinished façade is a high, severe wall of rough stone. The interior is prevalently 18th century; the Corsini Chapel, at the end of the left transept, by Silvani and Foggini, with ceiling frescoed by Luca Giordano with the *Apotheosis of St. Andrea Corsini* (1682) is a 17th century masterpiece. At the end of the opposite transept is the main feature of the church: the **Brancacci Chapel**, the decoration of which was commissioned in 1425 by Felice Brancacci, a rich Florentine merchant and diplomat from Masolino da Panicale, who still conformed to the Gothic taste, but was also open to the new ideas that were beginning to emerge in Tuscan painting at the time; and the pioneer, the great master of this renewal was the colleague Masolino chose to work with him on the Brancacci Chapel: Masaccio. The latter probably took the older painter's place in the following year, when Masolino was called to the court of Hungary, but for reasons unknown (perhaps his extreme poverty obliged

The church of Santa Maria del Carmine on Piazza del Carmine.

him to leave the city), he did not finish the work, which was completed by Filippino Lippi between 1481 and 1485. The best of Masaccio's brief career (he died in 1428 at the age of 27) is in the Brancacci Chapel: his frescoes won the unconditional admiration of Verrocchio, Fra Angelico, Leonardo, Botticelli, Perugino, Michelangelo and Raphael: his startling rediscovery of the classical laws of perspective which for the first time in Italian painting endows his figures with an almost sculptural solidity, the dramatically essential way in which he relates the episodes of the New and Old Testaments, recalls the superb simplicity of Giotto, but also make him the first great master of the Italian Renaissance. The cycles of illustrations on the walls of the Brancacci Chapel are two: *Original Sin* and *Scenes from the Life of St. Peter*; among the most significant are the *Expulsion from the Earthly Paradise*, a powerful masterpiece by Masaccio which faces the *Temptation of Adam and Eve*, by Masolino, on the wall opposite; *St Peter heals the lame man and restores Tabitha to life*, by both artists; *St. Peter baptises the Neophytes*, by Masaccio; *the Payment of the Tribute money*, and *St Peter heals the Sick*, also by Masaccio.

FOURTH ITINERARY

*Piazza del Duomo - Via Tornabuoni -
Strozzi Palace - Santa Trinità -
Palazzo Davanzati - Santa Maria Novella*

Via Tornabuoni, the most fashionable street in town.

Via dei Cerretani – One of the busiest thoroughfares in the city, this street goes from Piazza del Duomo to the main railroad station. A few yards from Piazza del Duomo it passes the **church of Santa Maria Maggiore**. First built in the 10th century, it was later rebuilt at the end of the 1200s. Over the portal is a sculpture of the *Virgin and Child* (14th century Pisan school). Inside is the tomb of *Brunetto Latini*, Dante's master. In the chapel to the left of the choir is a 13th century painted relief of the *Virgin Enthroned* attributed to Coppo di Marcovaldo. Continuing down Via dei Cerretani, we soon reach Via Rondinelli, on the left, which in turn leads into **Piazza Antinori**. The square is named for the elegant 15th century **Palazzo degli Antinori** on the right, attributed to Giuliano da Maiano. Opposite the palace is the **church of San Gaetano**. Originally a Romanesque structure, it was entirely rebuilt in the Florentine Baroque style by Matteo Nigetti, Gherardo and Pier Francesco Silvani. The aisleless interior is lined in black marble. In the second chapel on the left is the *Martyrdom of St. Laurence* painted by Pietro da Cortona.

Via Tornabuoni – This is Florence's most aristocratic street and one of the most beautiful in the world. Lining it are lovely old mansions, fine shops, and smart restaurants. On the right at Number 19 is **Palazzo Larderel**, a lovely late Renaissance building designed by Giovanni Antonio Dosio (1580). Opposite, at number 20, is **Palazzo Corsi**. It was restructured in 1875,

Palazzo Strozzi.

although the original construction was designed by Michelozzo whose elegant inner courtyard is still extant. **Palazzo Viviani**, formerly **Palazzo della Robbia** (number 15), was originally the home of the renowned della Robbia family. It was restructured in 1639 by G. B. Foggini.

Further on, to the left, we come upon the tawny bulk of *Palazzo Strozzi*.

STROZZI PALACE

Filippo Strozzi, a Florentine merchant of long-standing wealth (he had the merit of introducing into Tuscany not only the cultivation of artichokes, but also a good variety of fig), commissioned Benedetto da Maiano to build the palace in 1489; Benedetto was succeeded by Cronaca who directed the work until 1504. Later the construction was interrupted and resumed several times; the Strozzi family fell into disfavour in 1538, the palace was confiscated by Cosimo I dei Medici and given back 30 years later. Now it houses the Gabinetto Vieusseux and other cultural organisations; exhibitions are held here as well as the **biennial Antiques Exhibition Fair**. The massive building has a stone plinth all round it at the base, projecting like a bench; the exterior recalls that of Palazzo Medici-Riccardi, with pronounced rustication; at the top is a magnificent cornice by Cronaca; the two upper storeys have fine mullioned,twin-arched windows; there is a majestic courtyard inside, also by Cronaca.

Piazza Santa Trinità – Surrounded by noble mansions, the piazza is at the beginning of Via Tornabuoni, with the **Column of Justice** in the centre. This came from the Baths of Caracalla in Rome and supports the statue of *Justice* by Francesco del Tadda (1581). The fine large battlemented palace that extends as far as Lungarno Acciaioli is the 13th century **Palazzo Spini-Ferroni** (restored in the 19th century); at No. 1 of the piazza is **Palazzo Bartolini-Salimbeni**, Baccio d'Agnolo's masterpiece, with its unusual stone-cross partioned windows (1517-20). The western side of the square is occupied by the church of Santa Trinita.

Palazzo Spini-Ferroni.

The church of Santa Trinita.

CHURCH OF SANTA TRINITA

The church goes back to the 11th century; the Mannerist façade is by Buontalenti (1593-94); The **interior** contains important art works of the 14th and 15th centuries. Upon the inner façade you can see the remains of the original Romanesque church structure. Right aisle: on the altar of the right chapel *Virgin and Child with Saints* by Neri di Bicci. The fourth chapel was painted by Lorenzo Monaco and has Fra Angelico's *Scenes from the Life of Mary* and *Prophets* on the ceiling. On the altar is a panel painting of the *Annunciation*. The Sacristy (right transept) contains the magnificient *Tomb of Onofrio Strozzi* by Pietro di Niccolò Lamberti (1421). The second transept chapel to the right is the **Sassetti Chapel** with its famous frescoed cycle by Domenico Ghirlandaio (1483-1486).

Adoration of the Shepards, by Ghirlandaio (church of Santa Trinita).

Outside the chapel on the wall above the arch: *Statue of David* painted upon a tall column. Right: the *Tiburtine Sybil announcing the birth of Christ to Augustus*. Four *Sybils* on the ceiling of the chapel and *Episodes from the Life of St. Francis* on the side and end-walls.

Starting from the upper left: 1) *St. Francis giving up his earthly possessions*, 2) *Approval of the Franciscan Rule*, and 3) *The Trial by Fire before the Sultan*. The lower register starting from the left shows: 4) *St. Francis receiving the Stigmata*, to the right, 5) *the death of St. Francis*; on the wall behind the altar: 6) *St. Francis; invoked after his death, resuscitates a youthful member of the Spini family*. Below are portraits of Francesco Sassetti and his wife, Nera Corsi, who commissioned the work. One of Ghirlandaio's best-loved works, the *Adoration of the Sherpherds* (1495), is on the altar. The *tombs of Francesco and Nera Sassetti* attributed to Giuliano da Sangallo (1491) flank the altar. In the adjoining chapel is a huge *Crucifix*. It is known as the "Crucifix of St. Giovanni Gualberto". On the altar of the main chapel is an altarpiece with the *Holy Trinity and Saints* by Mariotto di Nardo (1416). In the left transept in the second chapel to the left of the main one, is the exquisite carved marble and majolica *tomb of Benozzo, Bishop of Fiesole* by Luca della Robbia. Fourth chapel on the left: 15th century Sienese school altarpiece with the *Coronation of the Virgin*. The third chapel contains a panel painting by Neri di Bicci of the *Annunciation* set on the altar. The walls are frescoed with the *Disputation of St. Catherine* by followers of Giotto.

Once outside the church, one turns right towards the Bridge of Santa Trinita. Built in 1252 and rebuilt several times, it now has the form given it by Bartolomeo Ammannati in 1567-70; at the ends are four statues of the *Seasons*, 1608. The most famous of these is the one representing *Spring*, by Pietro Francavilla (at the corner with Lungarno Acciaioli).

The bridge of Santa Trinita.

PALAZZO DAVANZATI

This stands in Via Porta Rossa, a narrow, picturesque street connecting Piazza Santa Trinita with Via Calzaioli, on Piazza Davanzati. The palace, one of the finest and best preserved of the 14th century, was built for the Davizzi family and passed in 1578 to the rich, powerful Davanzati family, who added various parts to it, including the loggia at the end; it now houses the interesting Museo dell'Antica Casa Fiorentina (Museum of the Ancient Florentine Home). Picturesque, porticoed courtyard, with a fine staircase leading up to the gallery round each storey. On the first floor is a hall with a fine cupboard for arms, and other furniture, a large table with an exquisite collection of caskets and some small 15th-16th century terracotta busts of the Florentine school; the delightful Parrot Room, with walls decorated with mock tapestry, with a fine 14th century fireplace; a small drawing room, with furniture and paintings of the 16th century; the beautiful Peacock Room, with decorated walls, a fine tabernacle (15th century) and a carved 16th century bedstead, which has a splendid and extremely rare white silk cover, embroidered with the *Story of Tristram* (14th century Sicilian work); on the second floor, a hall like the first, with 16th century furniture; a room of early 16th century Florentine paintings; a study with other 14th - 15th century paintings and two painted chests; the magnificent Nuptial Chamber, with 14th century frescoes, two tabernacles and a chest full of contemporary linen. Lastly, on the third floor, the kitchen containing various utensils, crockery, a small loom and a curious chandelier with oil lamps. Many of the rooms have fine wooden ceilings, some of which are beautifully decorated, and dressers containing 14th - 17th century pottery; there are also some "place of ease": little rooms with the old latrines. Some of the rooms in the basement of the palace are used for temporary exhibitions.

Behind Palazzo Davanzati, off the parallel street known as Borgo Santissimi Apostoli we find Piazza del Limbo, so called because it was probably used as the burial-ground for un-christened babies (whose souls, according to the Church's doctrine, ended up in Limbo). In this piazza is the **Church of the Holy Apostles**, erected in the 11th century and rebuilt in the 16th. It still has its fine stone Romanesque façade with a Latin inscription (apocryphal) attributing the foundation of the church to Charlemagne. The interior has a nave and two side aisles, and a fine trussed ceiling; in the third chapel on the right is an *Immaculate Conception* by Vasari; on the high altar a fine 14th century polyptych; in the left aisle a large glazed terracotta *tabernacle* by Giovanni della Robbia and the tomb of Oddo Altoviti, by Benedetto da Rovezzano.

From piazza Santa Trinita, one takes Via del Parione and after crossing piazza Goldoni, one comes to Borgognissanti, leading into piazza Ognissanti, where the **Church of Ognissanti** (All Saints), with its pleasant Baroque façade by Matteo Nigetti (1637) stands, overlooking the Arno. The church was restructured in the 17th century. The bell-tower is 14th century. Inside the *Madonna of Mercy* frescoed by Ghirlandaio, commissioned by the Vespucci family (the future great navigator Amerigo also appears in it; 1472), as well as the detached frescoes of *St. Jerome in his study*, by Ghirlandaio and *St. Augustine in his study* by Botticelli. The famous **Last Supper** by Ghirlandaio is in the **refectory**, left of the church.

Back once more in piazza Goldoni, one turns left into Via dei Fossi, that leads up to spacious piazza Santa Maria Novella, emerging into it at the corner of the Loggia of St. Paul (c. 1490), decorated with della Robbia terracottas. On the other side of the square we can admire the luminous façade of the great Dominican church of Santa Maria Novella, first designed by the architect friars Fra Sisto and Fra Ristoro.

Aerial view of the church of Santa Maria Novella on its beautiful square.

SANTA MARIA NOVELLA

The façade was begun in 1300, and the lower part was finished before the middle of the century, in the typical Florentine Romanesque - Gothic style. After the middle of the 15th century, Leon Battista Alberti, the great 15th century theorist of architecture, completed the inlaid marble façade by adding the central doorway and the upper part, of extraordinary elegance, with a rose window, tympanum and side scrolls. The **interior** in the Cistercian Gothic style in the "softened" form that this style took in Italy; it is in the form of a Latin cross, with nave and side aisles and composite columns; an incredible number of works of art decorate the walls and chapels. In the second bay of the right aisle is the *tomb of the Blessed Villana*, by Bernardo Rossellino (1451). The right transept leads to the Rucellai Chapel; on the altar is a *Madonna* by Nino Pisano, in the floor the *tombstone of*

The Spaniards Chapel.

Leonardo Dati, by Ghiberti (1425). The chapel of Filippo Strozzi to the right of the high altar is covered with frescoes by Filippino Lippi (c. 1500) with *Stories of Sts. Philip and John the Evangelist*. The **chapel of the main altar** was frescoed by Domenico Ghirlandaio (c. 1495; young Michelangelo was probably one of his assistants) with beautiful *Scenes of the Life of the Virgin and St. John the Baptist*. The Gondi Chapel (left of the **main chapel**) has the celebrated *Crucifix* by Brunelleschi. In the Strozzi Chapel (left transept) are frescoes by Nardo di Cione (c. 1367: remarkable representation of *Hell*). In the Sacristy nearby is a Crucifix, a youthful work by Giotto. Lastly, at the third bay of the left aisle, the marvellous **Trinity** by Masaccio (c. 1427) and the pulpit designed by Brunelleschi. Outside the church, to the right, is the interesting group of cloisters. The 14th century **Green Cloister** has frescoes in the lunettes by 15th century painters including Paolo Uccello, who painted the *Scenes from the Genesis* (a very fine *Flood*, c. 1430); the **Spaniards' Chapel** opens onto the cloister, frescoed in the 14th cent. by Andrea di Bonaiuto, and used in the 16th cent. by Eleonora di Toledo's Spanish courtiers.

Above: the Birth of the Virgin, by Ghirlandaio; *below:* detail from the Ghirlandaio frescoes and one of the halls in the Santa Maria Novella Cloisters.

85

FIFTH ITINERARY

Piazza del Duomo - Church and Museum of San Marco - Gallery of the Academy - Santissima Annunziata - Hospital of the Innocents - Archaeological Museum

Piazza San Marco with the church of San Marco in the background.

Via Cavour, one of the busiest thoroughfares in town, is flanked by severe 17th and 18th century mansions that give it a very stately appearance. It links piazza del Duomo with piazza della Libertà, traversing the left side piazza of San Marco, which has a prevalently recently built appearance; the only medieval note is the 14th century loggia of the Accademia, once part of the former Hospital of St. Matthew, and now the entrance portico of the **Academy of Fine Arts**. On the corner with Via degli Arazzieri is the *Palace of Livia* (1775), built by Grand Duke Pietro Leopoldo for a circus dancer, Livia Malfatti. In the centre of the piazza are shrubs and trees and a *monument to General Manfredo Fanti*, by Pio Fedi (1873). One side of the piazza is occupied by the **church** and **monastery of San Marco**. There was a monastery of Silvestrini monks here from 1299 onwards; in the first half of the 15th century Cosimo the Elder assigned both the church and the monastery to the reformed Dominican monks of the Blessed Giovanni Dominici; this was partly by desire of Pope Eugene IV, and partly in expiation of Cosimo's own misdeeds. He commissioned Michelozzo to carry out the work of restoration, and invested 40,000 florins in it. In the following centuries there were several alterations, particularly to the church, which has an 18th century neo-Renaissance façade. The interior was re-structured by Giambologna in 1588 and by Silvani in 1678; on the interior façade is a *Crucifix* by followers of Giotto; at the third altar on the right, a *Virgin in prayer* (mosaic).

MUSEUM OF SAN MARCO

The entrance to the monastery of San Marco is beside the church. This was one of the most important centres in Florence in the 15th century, not only because of the protection granted to it by Cosimo the Elder and Lorenzo the Magnificent, but also because of the unquestioned authority of its prior, St. Antoninus, and the fact that Savonarola, Fra Angelico and Fra Bartolomeo lived there. Fra Angelico was one of the greatest artists of the 15th century; he infused Masaccio's newly rediscovered rules of perspective with a spirit that was still Gothic, to express a mystical, contemplative religious experience. The **Cloister of St. Antoninus**, by Michelozzo, has frescoed lunettes and there are some interesting rooms opening on to it. The **Pilgrims' Hospice** contains an exceptional series of panel paintings by Fra Angelico: the *Linen-merchant's tabernacle*, the *Altar-piece from the Convent of Bosco ai Frari*, the *Annalena altar-piece*, the *Descent from the Cross*, the *Last Judgement*. The **Chapter-house** contains a magnificent *Crucifixion* by Fra Angelico. The artist also decorated the **Dormitory** on the first floor; each cell is adorned by master pieces, like the *Annunciation*, *Noli me tangere*, the *Transfiguration* and the *Coronation of the Virgin*. In the Prior's Apartment is a *Portrait of Savonarola*, who lived in these rooms, by Fra Bartolomeo.

Angel Musicians, by Fra Angelico (Museum of St. Mark's).

Deposition from the Cross, by Fra Angelico (Museum of St. Mark's).

GALLERY OF THE ACADEMY

This is one of the most famous galleries in Italy, visited by thousands of people, especially owing to the presence of the **David** and of other famous sculptures by Michelangelo. The Gallery, (Via Ricasoli 60, near Piazza San Marco) was founded in 1784 by Grand Duke Peter Leopold of Hapsburg Lorraine, as an Academy of Fine Arts, to unite all the schools of art, drawing and sculpture already existing in the city; the gallery was thus created with the specific purpose of helping the pupils to know and to study the Old Masters. Many of the works, however, came from a previous collection, that belonged to the Academy of the Art of Drawing, an institution of great prestige, founded in 1562 by Cosimo I. This included all the greatest artists of the time, and was based on the

Michelangelo's David in the Tribuna of the Academy Gallery.

Michelangelo's Pietà (Deposition) and St. Matthew (Academy Gallery).

14th century Company of Painters of St. Luke. The already considerable collection of paintings was increased as a result of the suppression of churches and monasteries (1786 and 1808); there were further acquisitions and in 1873 the *David* was brought here, followed in 1911 by the *Prisoners* and *St. Matthew*, while the *Pietà* only arrived in 1939, when it was bought by the State. The Gallery also exhibits a plaster model by Giambologna as well as a notable collection of paintings from the 13th till the early 16th century; among the most important works are: a *Crucifix*, Sienese school,

Left: **Jesus entering Jerusalem, by Santi di Tito;** *right*: **Madonna and Child, by A. Botticelli (Academy Gallery).**

second half of the 13th century (attributed by some people to the great Duccio di Buoninsegna); the *Tree of the Cross*, by Pacino di Buonaguida (early 14th century); a polyptych by Andrea Orcagna (mid 14th century) and works by his brothers, including a triptych by Nardo di Cione (1365) and a *Coronation of the Virgin* by Jacopo di Cione; 24 panels by Taddeo Gaddi (14 with *Scenes of the Life of Christ* and 10 with *Scenes of the life of St. Francis*; the very fine *Pietà* by Giovanni da Milano (1365); the *Adimari Chest*; a *Visitation* attributed to Domenico Ghirlandaio; the *Madonna of the Sea* and the youthful *Madonna and Child, little St. John and two Angels*, by Sandro Botticelli; *Trinity and Saints*, by Alesso Baldovinetti (1471).

Going back to Piazza San Marco, we turn right into Via Cesare Battisti which leads into Piazza **Santissima Annunziata**. This elegant square is surrounded on three sides by porticos; on the right, the **Hospital of the Innocents**; at right angles, the **church of the Santissima Annunziata**: The entrance to the **Archaeological Museum** is at No. 38, Via Colonna (on the left), which exits from the square between the church and the Hospital, beneath the arch. Left, the **Palace of the Servants of Mary**, designed to resemble the Hospital of the Innocents by Antonio da Sangallo and Baccio d'Agnolo. The building on the corner of Via dei Servi on the left is **Palazzo Grifoni**, by Ammannati (1563). In the centre is the statue of *Grand Duke Ferdinando I* begun by Giambologna and finished by Tacca (1608).

Piazza Santissima Annunziata, with the church of the Santissima Annunziata on the left.

SANTISSIMA ANNUNZIATA

In 1250 seven young Florentines, later beatified as the Seven Saints, founded the order of the Servites, or Servants of Mary, and began to build a shrine dedicated to the Virgin. The church was rebuilt by Michelozzo in the 15th century, and later by Antonio Manetti who, together with Leon Battista Alberti, was responsible for the design of the circular choir at the end of the aisleless nave. The porch on the piazza is late 16th century. Between this and the church is the **Cloister of Vows**, decorated with fine early 16th century frescoes by Andrea del Sarto, Pontormo, Rosselli, Franciabigio and other Mannerists, to the left of the entrance, just inside the church, which was restored and embellished in the Baroque period, is a small 15th century *Temple*, that contains a greatly venerated 14th century Florentine school *Annunciation*, which is supposed to have been partly painted by an angel. Among the many works of art, mention should be made of two lecterns in the form of eagles (15th century English work) in the elegant Tribune; *Jesus and St. Julian* by Andrea del Castagno (c. 1455, first altar on the left) and the *Trinity* by the same (second altar on the left). Beside the church are the buildings of the Monastery which include the **Cloister of the Dead**.

The Andrea della Robbia tondi on the Hospital of the Innocents' façade.

HOSPITAL OF THE INNOCENTS

In 1419 the Guild of Silk Merchants decided to purchase a piece of land and build a hospital for the foundlings or "Innocents". Brunelleschi was commissioned to provide the plan, which determined the architecture of the whole piazza on which the hospital faces, creating a portico whose proportions, in relation to the rest, required the uniformity of all the surrounding buildings. We can see here how the Renaissance conception of "planning" was replacing the casual building that went on in the Middle Ages, when one building was put up beside another in a completely different style. The hospital was finished in 1457; the front consists of nine wide arches on columns that stand at the top of a flight of steps; above these, a low upper storey which has windows with tympanums; between the arches, *glazed terracotta putti* (babies) by Andrea della Robbia (c. 1487); two pilaster strips close the portico at the sides. Inside: the cloisters by Brunelleschi and a collection of works mostly of the 15th century. The collection includes: an *Annunciation* by Giovanni del Biondo; *Adoration of the Magi* by Ghirlandaio (1488); a *Madonna and Child with Angels* by the school of Perugino; the *Madonna of the Innocents*, attributed to Pontormo and a *St. Sebastian* by Andrea del Sarto.

Mater Matuta (Archaeological Museum).

ARCHAEOLOGICAL MUSEUM

Cosimo the Elder was a keen collector of coins, goldsmiths' work and antique sculpture, a passion shared by the later Medici. The Hapsburg Lorraine family started the Egyptian antiquities section and encouraged independent excavation; in 1828 Leopold II subsidized an archaeological expedition in Egypt and Nubia led by the Frenchman Champollion and the Italian Rossellini. In 1880 the collection was housed in its present seat, Palazzo della Crocetta in Via della Colonna, built by Giulio Parigi in 1620. The museum is divided into three sections: the Etrurian Topographical Museum, the Etrusco-Graeco-Roman Antiquities, and the Egyp-

The Chimaera (Archaeological Museum).

tian Collection. On the ground floor are two rooms arranged
didactically: the famous François vase and the *Mater Matuta* are
kept here. The pleasant garden contains reconstructions, partly
with authentic materials, of funeral monuments and Etruscan
tombs. The Egyptian Collection is on the first floor. Among the
most interesting exhibits: the two *statuettes of handmaidens* intent
on domestic work; the statue of *Thutmosis* III (1490-1436 B.C.); the
"Fayyum" *portrait of a woman* (2nd century A.D.); painted slabs,
pillars, sarcophagi, mummies and a *war chariot*. Also on the first
floor, among the Antiquities, Attic *kouroi* of the 6th century B.C.;
Etruscan funeral urns; the statue of the *Orator* (c. 100 B.C.);
Etruscan sarcophagi; the *Chimaera of Arezzo*; the *Little Idol*; Attic
vases and Etruscan *buccheri*.

95

Leaving the Museum and turning right down Via della Colonna, one encounters Benvenuto Cellini's house, near the intersection with Via della Pergola. Here the great goldsmith-sculptor modelled and cast the famous *Perseus*, still standing under the Loggia in Piazza della Signoria. The street leads into a pleasantly landscaped square, Piazza d'Azeglio. Turning right into Via Farini we come to the **Synagogue** of Florence at number 6. Funded by David Levi's donation to the Jewish University, it was designed by a team of architects (Mariano Falcini, Marco Treves, and Vincenzo Micheli) and built between 1872 and 1874.

Overall view of the Sinagogue.

SIXTH ITINERARY

*Piazza del Duomo - Bargello Museum -
Badia Fiorentina - Buonarroti House -
Church and Museum of Santa Croce -
Horne Museum - Bardini Museum*

Piazza San Firenze.

Via del Proconsolo, which leads from Piazza del Duomo to piazza San Firenze, contains a number of interesting buildings, as well as the Bargello and the Badia, N° 10 is the **Pazzi Palace**, built between 1462 and 1472 for this family, who soon afterwards plotted the famous conspiracy against the Medici. At N° 12 is the **Unfinished Palace**, built by Buontalenti for the Strozzi family from 1592. This now houses the **Museum of Anthropology and Ethnology**, founded by Paolo Mantegazza in 1869, the first of its kind in Italy. Among the most interesting things are: the wooden statue of a native of Patagonia, ordered by the Grand Duke of Tuscany at the end of the 18th century, (it is over eight feet high, as it was modelled according to the fanciful description given at the time by a sea-captain; African handicrafts; the wooden sculptures of the mysterious people, the Kaffirs (Karakorum); Amazonian ornaments; an Eskimo kayak; masks from Oceania; arms from Malay; mummies of the Incas and religious objects from Tibet. A side street off Via del Proconsolo leads to the **House of Dante**, a medieval building restored in the 19th century, which is part of a group of houses that belonged to the Alighieri family; the museum has an ample documentation on 14th century Florence, including portraits of the poet and some rare editions of the *Divine Comedy*. Not far from piazza della Signoria, is the odd-shaped, fairly narrow piazza San Firenze,

97

dominated by two large buildings of differing styles and periods: **Palazzo Gondi**, by Giuliano da San Gallo (1490-1501), and, opposite, the great Baroque complex of the ex-Convent of San Firenze (17th-18th centuries): the left side is the church dedicated to St. Filippo Neri, called **San Firenze**, the right side is the seat of the Tribunal of Justice of Florence.

NATIONAL MUSEUM (BARGELLO)

This is the most important Italian museum of sculpture and minor arts. It is housed in the severe square Bargello palace, a 13th century building of great historical importance, that was begun in 1255 and was first used as the seat of the Captain of the People. After 1574 it was the seat of the Captain of Justice, called the Bargello (that is the chief of police) and the palace became grimly famous for the executions held there. The Museum was founded in 1865. A description of the principal works must begin with the splendid **courtyard**, under the arches of which there is a large and very fine cannon of the early 17th century and, among the

The Bargello Courtyard.

David, by Donatello.

David, by Verrocchio.

Abraham about to sacrifice
Isaac, by L. Ghiberti.

Abraham about to sacrifice
Isaac, by F. Brunelleschi.

sculptures, the delightful *Fisherboy* by Vincenzo Gemito (1877).
One of the rooms on the ground floor contains masterpieces by
Michelangelo such as the bust of *Brutus* (c. 1540), who was seen at
that time as a heroic liberator from tyranny; the so-called *Pitti
tondo* (c. 1504), rendered with the characteristic and expressive

Madonna of the Capucin Nuns', by Luca della Robbia and workshop (Bargello).

"unfinished" style; the *David-Apollo* (c. 1531), delicate and harmonious; the youthful *Drunken Bacchus* (1497-99); among other works, another *Bacchus* by Sansovino (1520) and the bronze bust of *Cosimo I*, by Benvenuto Cellini (1546-57) as well as Giambologna's famous *Mercury*. On the first floor, on the fine balcony are more bronzes by Giambologna; in the Donatello Hall, besides masterpieces by the great 15th century sculptor, are numerous terracottas by Luca della Robbia and the panels with the *Sacrifice of Isaac* by Brunelleschi and Ghiberti; in the other rooms, splendid majolicas from Faenza and other provenances, enamels, goldsmiths' work, liturgical objects, valuable ivories of various periods. On the second floor: a room with terracottas by Giovanni della Robbia and one with those by Andrea della Robbia; a room devoted to Verrocchio, that also contains works by Rossellino, Pollaiolo and others; lastly, two rooms with small bronzes and arms.

The Cloister of the Orange Trees (Badia Fiorentina).

BADIA FIORENTINA

Opposite the Bargello, in Via del Proconsolo, is the entrance to the church of the Badia. Founded in the 10th century, it was rebuilt at the end of the 13th, perhaps by Arnolfo di Cambio, and again in 1627. The elegant hexagonal **bell-tower** is 14th century. The fine 15th-16th century doorway leads into a porticoed courtyard, where the entrance to the church is. To the left of the entrance is a masterpiece by Filippo Lippi, *the Madonna appears to St. Bernard* (c. 1485); in the right transept is the *monument to Bernardo Giugni*, by Mino da Fiesole (c. 1470); in the opposite transept, by the same sculptor, is the *monument to Count Ugo* (1469-81) whose mother founded the Badia. To the right of the presbytery is the entrance to the Sacristy, from which one goes out into the **Cloister "of the Orange Trees"** built in 1435-40 by Bernardo Rossellino; this quiet, elegant cloister has two orders of arches; the lunettes in the upper gallery are frescoed with scenes from the *Life of St. Benedict*, a 15th century work attributed to the Portuguese painter, Giovanni di Consalvo.

Via Ghibellina starts at the corner with Via del Proconsolo, outside the church of the Badia Fiorentina. At No. 70 we find the Buonarroti House.

BUONARROTI HOUSE

This 15th century building is not the birthplace of Michelangelo, who was born to a noble family of Florentine origin on March 6th 1475 at Caprese, in the Casentino district; his father had been sent there to act as mayor. The house in Florence was bought by

Madonna of the Stairs and Wooden Crucifix, by Michelangelo
(Buonarroti House).

Michelangelo, who never lived there, for his nephew Leonardo. Subsequently Michelangelo Buonarroti the Younger, the artist's great nephew and a distinguished man of letters, had the house redecorated, commissioning some of the best known painters in early 17th century Florence, including Giovanni da San Giovanni, Empoli, Matteo Rosselli, Francesco Furini and Artemisia Gentileschi, to paint scenes of the glorification of Michelangelo. The rooms contain works by Michelangelo, including first works, drawings, models and sketches. Of interest: portraits of members of the Buonarroti family, and a predella with *Stories of St. Nicholas of Bari*, by Giovanni di Francesco (15th century), a *Narcissus* attributed to Paolo Uccello, and a *Love Scene*, an early work by Titian.

Opposite Casa Buonarroti, Via delle Pinzochere leads into Piazza **Santa Croce**. From the Middle Ages this piazza was the scene of festivities, tournaments, meetings, games; such as the famous tournament between Lorenzo and Giuliano dei Medici; St. Bernardino da Siena preached here, and the traditional football in costume is still played here. In 1865 Enrico Pazzi placed the monument to Dante (later transferred to the front of the church) in the middle of the square. On the south side of the piazza is **Palazzo dell'Antella**, the façade of which, on corbels, was frescoed in the space of three weeks by twenty painters directed by Giovanni di San Giovanni (17th century); above the door is a bust of Cosimo II; between two windows on the ground floor is a 16th century marble disc indicating the centre of the piazza for the football game.

The church of Santa Croce (Holy Cross) on its spacious square.

SANTA CROCE

This church originated as a small oratory, built here by a community of monks in 1228. In 1294 Arnolfo di Cambio began the construction of the present basilica, in the monumental, soberly decorated style, that characterises Franciscan churches. The church was consecrated in 1443 in the presence of Pope Eugene IV. In 1566 Giorgio Vasari, commissioned by Cosimo I, designed the altars in the side aisles; this involved destroying the old choir and numerous frescoes. The **façade** of the church was only added in the mid 19th century and was designed by Niccolò Matas (like the bell-tower built by Gaetano Baccani in 1847). The extraordinary importance of this church, with its numerous works of art, is enhanced by the many tombs of illustrious men (the "Urns of the Strong" celebrated by Ugo Foscolo in the *Sepolcri*.) The **interior** has a nave and two side aisles, with pointed arches supported by octagonal stone pillars. The floor contains no fewer than 276 tombstones, the oldest being 14th century. In the central nave, at the third pillar on the right, is the fine marble *pulpit* by Benedetto

Above: the interior of Santa Croce; *below*: the right aisle, with the tomb of Michelangelo in the foreground.

The High Altar with the frescoed Golden Legend cycle by Agnolo Gaddi (Santa Croce).

da Maiano (1472-76); the square panels relate *Episodes from the Life of St. Francis*. In the right aisle, at the first pillar, the *Madonna of the Milk* by Rossellino (1478); opposite, the *funeral monument to Michelangelo* by Vasari and helpers (1570); the crouching female

Left: **the tomb of Galileo Galilei;** *right:* **detail of Giotto's frescoed Stories from the Life of St. Francis of Assisi** (Santa Croce).

figures represent the Muses of Painting, Sculpture and Architecture; next come the *Cenotaph of Dante Alighieri* (buried at Ravenna) by Stefano Ricci (1829); the *tomb of Vittorio Alfieri,* by Canova in 1810; the *tomb of Niccolò Machiavelli,* by Spinazzi (1787); the splendid *Annunciation* by Donatello (c. 1435); the *monument to Leonardo Bruni,* by Rossellino (c. 1444); the *tombs of Gioacchino Rossini and Ugo Foscolo.* In the right transept, on the right, is the Castellani chapel, frescoed about 1385 by Agnolo Gaddi with *Stories of St. Nicholas of Bari, John the Baptist,* and *Anthony Abbot.* At the end of the transept is the entrance to the Baroncelli Chapel, frescoed with *Stories of the Virgin* by Taddeo Gaddi; on the altar a polyptych with the *Coronation of the Virgin,* from the workshop of Giotto. At the corner of the transept is the entrance to the fine 14th century **Sacristy;** on the right wall, three episodes from the *Passion* by Taddeo Gaddi and others; in the end wall is the entrance to the Rinuccini Chapel, with frescoes by Giovanni da Milano. Returning to the church one should visit the chapels along the transept; the Peruzzi Chapel (fourth from the right) has splendid frescoes by Giotto with *Stories of the Baptist* and *St. John the Evangelist;* the Bardi Chapel (the fifth) has *Stories of St. Francis,* also by Giotto; this cycle is to be placed among the

The Pazzi Chapel, in the Museum of Santa Croce.

painter's masterpieces (c. 1325); the Chapel of the High Altar has frescoes by Agnolo Gaddi and a polyptych by Niccolò Gerini (end of 14th century). Of the left transept chapels, the Bardi di Vernio Chapel has fine *Stories of St. Sylvester*, by Maso di Banco (c. 1340). The Bardi Chapel at the end of the transept has a *Crucifix* by Donatello (c. 1425). On the left, the Salviati Chapel with the 19th century tomb of Sofia Zamoyski by Lorenzo Bartolini. In the left aisle, another series of funeral monuments; among others, the *tomb of Galileo Galilei* by Giulio Foggini (18th century).

SANTA CROCE MUSEUM

Housed in part of the Monastery of Santa Croce: the entrance is to the right of the church. The first, and most important is the old 14th century Refectory; the end wall is covered by an enormous fresco by Taddeo Gaddi representing the *Tree of Life*, the *Last Supper* and other scenes; on the right wall is the magnificent *Crucifix* painted on wood by Cimabue, badly damaged by the 1966 flood and three fragments of the *Triumph of Death* frescoed by Orcagna on the walls of Santa Croce (they were found under

The famous Cimabue Crucifix (Museum of Santa Croce).

Vasari's altars, and detached); on the left is the *St. Ludovic* in gilded bronze by Donatello (1423). The remains of 14th and 15th century glass windows. Other works by Andrea del Castagno, Agnolo Bronzino, Giorgio Vasari, etc. in the other rooms. The harmonious façade of the **Pazzi chapel** acts as back-drop to the first cloister. Filippo Brunelleschi designed the building c. 1430; he worked on it at intervals until 1444. A pronaos preceding the entrance has six Corinthian columns and a wide central arch between elegant inset panels in grey sandstone; the frieze with *heads of cherubs* is by Desiderio da Settignano. The chapel's dome has a conical covering (1461) and under the portico the smaller dome is decorated with glazed terracotta, by Luca della Robbia; by the same, the Tondo of St. Andrew above the door, the panels of which are splendidly carved by Giuliano da Maiano (1472). The rectangular interior has the clarity and measured rhythm of the best creations of Brunelleschi: white walls, grooved pilaster strips in grey stone, wide arches and the brilliantly coloured tondi by Luca della Robbia, with figures of *Apostles* and *Evangelists*. In the presbytery, a stained glass panel attributed to Alessio Baldovinetti and a small dome with Signs of the Zodiac. Brunelleschi's Great Cloister is through the door, left, leaving the Chapel.

Leaving Santa Croce, we turn left into Via Magliabechi. Along the left side of the street is the west wing of the **Biblioteca Nazionale** (State Library) [entrance on Piazza Cavalleggeri]. This is Italy's most important library with priceless manuscripts and historical documents. At the end of Corso Tintori, the street intersecting Via Magliabechi, we turn left into Via de' Benci. The first building on the left, number 6, is **Palazzo degli Alberti e dei Corsi** attributed to Giuliano da Sangallo, now the Horne Museum.

HORNE MUSEUM

At the beginning of this century Herbert Percy Horne gathered together a fine collection of furniture, pictures, sculptures and other objects, in a beautiful 15th century mansion in Via dei Benci that belonged to the Alberti family. Among the principal works, which the English collector donated to the Italian State, are: a stucco *Madonna* by Antonio Rossellino; a fine *Holy Family* by Beccafumi; the splendid early 15th century inlaid sacristy bench; *Madonna and Saints* by Lorenzo Monaco; the *Allegory of Music* by Dosso Dossi; a *Madonna* and a *Pietà* both attributed to Simone Martini; the fragment of a polyptych by Pietro Lorenzetti; the magnificent *St. Stephen* by Giotto; the figure of *Esther* by Filippino Lippi: the fragment of a *story of St. Julian* by Masaccio; drawings, coins, majolicas and cutlery.

Continuing down Via dei Benci towards the Arno we come to the bridge known as Ponte alle Grazie. After crossing the bridge, we continue a few yards in the same direction to Piazza Mozzi. Number 1 is the Bardini Museum.

BARDINI MUSEUM

This collection, constituted at the beginning of this century by the antiquarian Stefano Bardini, is housed in the fine 19th century Bardini Palace. Left to the Commune of Florence in 1923, the museum still has the character of a rich private collection; the rooms are full of furniture, paintings, sculpture, weapons, tapestries and works of art and craftsmanship of various periods and origins. Among the principal works are a *Madonna and Child* attributed to Lucas Cranach the Elder; *Charity*, by Tino di Camaino (early 14th century); splendid 16th-17th century Persian carpets; a bas-relief of the *Virgin and Child with Angels*, attributed to Donatello; a series of 15th century chests; a fine *St. Michael the Archangel* by Antonio del Pollaiolo. On the second floor of the palace is the interesting **Corsi gallery**, a collection of works of art ranging from the twelfth to the nineteenth century.

The Michelangelo monument in the middle of Piazzale Michelangelo.

PIAZZALE MICHELANGELO

On the other side of the Arno, one climbs up the Viale dei Colli, that winds its way for almost six chilometres along the hills lying south of the town (one can also take the shorter route of the Rampe that start at Porta San Niccolò), until one reaches the wide viewpoint or terrace that surveys the whole town, spread out in the valley, and the surrounding hillsides: piazzale Michelangelo. This splendid esplanade, together with the beautiful Viale dei Colli, was planned by Giuseppe Poggi in the 1860s, as a spectacular climax to his great rearrangement of Florence, at that time capital of Italy. In the centre of the square is the monument to Michelangelo cast in 1875 with copies in bronze of some of his marble statues. Going on up the hill, behind Piazzale Michelangelo, is the little **church of San Salvatore al Monte**.

View of the town from Piazzale Michelangelo.

SAN MINIATO AL MONTE

One of the oldest and most beautiful churches in Florence. A wide marble staircase leads up to it from the Viale Galileo-section of the Viale dei Colli. An ancient 4th century oratory, dedicated to St. Miniato, reputedly the first Christian martyr of Florence, was incorporated into the 11th-13th century Romanesque church. The flowing succession of arches and geometrical patterns on the façade are in green and white marble. The fine mosaic in the centre (13th century, much restored) represents *Christ between the Virgin and St. Miniato*; at the top of the tympanum, *the Eagle*, the symbol of the Guild of Woolmerchants who subsidized the upkeep of the church. The **interior** has a nave and two side aisles, with a crypt and a raised presbytery above it; the floor of the nave is paved with splendid inlaid marble panels. In the centre, between the two flights of steps leading up to the presbytery, is the *Crucifix Chapel*, by Michelozzo (1448), commissioned by Piero the Gouty, the father of Lorenzo the Magnificent with a delightful multi-coloured majolica vault by Luca della Robbia and altar panels by Agnolo Gaddi. From the left aisle one enters the *Chapel of the Cardinal of Portugal*, one of the most elegant creations of the

111

The façade of the Basilica of San Miniato al Monte.

Florentine Renaissance, by Antonio Manetti (1461-66) a pupil of Brunelleschi; this contains the tomb of Jacopo Di Lusitania, archbishop of Lisbon, by Rossellino; fine della Robbia terracottas on the vault, a splendid *Annunciation* by Baldovinetti (on the left) and two *angels* frescoed by Antonio and Piero del Pollaiolo (on the wall opposite the entrance, above the copy of the *Saints Eustace, James and Vincent* by the Pollaiolo brothers, now at the Uffizi). On the vault of the crypt, above the altar, are frescoes of *Saints and Prophets* by Taddeo Gaddi. The presbytery of the church is surrounded with fine 13th century marble parapets and a splendid *pulpit*; on the right altar is a painting on wood by Jacopo del Casentino with *St. Miniato and eight scenes of his life*; the mosaic in the apse represents *Christ enthroned between the Virgin, St. Miniato and the symbols of the Evangelists* (1279, but restored in 1491 by Baldovinetti). From the Presbytery one turns right into the

Interior of the Basilica of San Miniato al Monte.

Sacristy, frescoed after 1387 by Spinello Aretino, with *Stories of St. Benedict*. To the right of the church is the Bishops' Palace (13th-14th century). Round the church are the walls of the Fortress constructed by Michelangelo in 1529 to defend Florence while it was being besieged by the Spanish army of Charles V.

Via San Leonardo – One of the most charming country roads leading off the Viale dei Colli. Along the flag-stoned road, the grey-green olive trees peep over the old stone walls and lovely villas, surrounded by cypresses in the traditional Tuscan manner. Halfway down, on the right, is a charming Romanesque church, **San Leonardo in Arcetri**, inside which are 14th century Tuscan school paintings and a Romanesque *marble pulpit* (early 13th century). The road ends at **Forte Belvedere** which was built between 1590 and 1595 by Giovanni de' Medici and Bernardo Buontalenti. Its ramparts command a superb view of the city below. Important art shows and other cultural events are periodically held here.

Above: the Belvedere or St. George Fortress; *below*: the Hapsburg Arch in Piazza della Libertà.

Overall view of Piazza Mino in Fiesole.

FIESOLE

A charming little town about 4 miles north of Florence, it was
founded by the Etruscans towards the 4th cent. B.C.; it was
destroyed and colonized by the Romans during the 1st cent.
B.C..After the fall of the Empire it was an important bishopric; in
the 12th century it succumbed to its stronger neighbour, Florence.
In the 15th cent., having lost all its political power, it became a
favourite summer resort for rich Florentines (the Medicis also had
a villa there) and, in the 19th century, foreign visitors, especially
the English also settled there. The centre of the little town is
Piazza Mino, where the principal public buildings are. The
Cathedral was built in 1028 and later enlarged in 1256 and 1300; in
the Salutati Chapel are frescoes by Cosimo Rosselli and the tomb
of Bishop Leonardo Salutati, by Mino da Fiesole, 15th century; on
the High Altar is a triptych by Bicci di Lorenzo (c. 1440); in the

Above: the Roman Amphitheatre; *below*: Roman "Penates" portraits from the Archaeological Museum (Fiesole).

crypt, which is Romanesque, are 15th century frescoes by Benedetto di Nanni, a baptismal font by Francesco del Tadda (16th century) and the wooden Bishop's Chair by Andrea Corsini (14th century). The **Bandini Museum** nearby has interesting Della Robbia terracottas and works by Agnolo and Taddeo Gaddi, Lorenzo Monaco and Jacopo del Sellaio. Also in Piazza Mino is the Praetorian Palace (15th century) with façade and loggia covered with coats of arms. Near the piazza is the **Roman theatre** (1st century B.C.) which seats an audience of 3000 and is still in use for summer concerts and other events. In the vicinity of the theatre are the remains of a temple (first Etruscan and later

The church and the monastery of St. Francis (Fiesole).

Roman) and some Roman baths. The **Archaeological Museum** beside the area of excavation contains relics of Etruscan and Roman Fiesole; urns from Chiusi and Volterra; storied stelae, typical of the zone; Greek vases, objects in *bucchero*, small bronzes. Returning to the piazza, one goes up a very steep little road to **Sant'Alessandro**, an ancient church standing on the site of an Etruscan temple. A little beyond it are the church and **monastery of San Francesco**; this church was built between the 14th and 15th century, and has a simple façade with a rose-window and porched entrance. The interior is Gothic with a single nave; the High Altar has a beautiful *Annunciation* by Raffaellino del Garbo (early 16th century); at the second altar on the left, *Madonna and Saints* by the school of Perugino; next to it, an *Immaculate Conception* by Cosimo Rosselli; a fine early 16th century inlaid choir. Right of the church is the **small Cloister of St. Bernardino** (13th-14th century). Half way between Fiesole and Florence is the **church of San Domenico** built in the 15th century but restored in the 17th; it contains a *Madonna and Child with Angels and Saints* by Fra Angelico (c. 1430) who was prior of the nearby monastery. Via di Badia dei Roccettini goes down from San Domenico to the **Badia Fiesolana**. The Cathedral of Fiesole in the early Middle Ages, the church was restored by the Camaldolese monks in the 11th century; the small, magnificent Romanesque façade belongs to this period. In 1456 the interior was restored by order of Cosimo the Elder, who lived here, and here assembled part of his collection of manuscripts, now kept in the Laurentian Library.

USEFUL INFORMATION

The last pages of the guide contain practical information on museums, hotels, public and private transport facilities and other useful hints for a visitor in Florence.
Various sign-posts along the main tourist itineraries make it easier to get to the more important museums and monuments.

EMERGENCY TELEPHONE NUMBERS

Police and General Emergency - ☎ 113
Carabinieri Emergency Squad - ☎ 112
ACI (Automobile Assistance) - ☎ 666500 - ☎ 116
State of the Roads - ☎ 4212
Galileo Galilei Airport (Pisa) - ☎ 050/28088-48219
Peretola Airport - ☎ 370123/370313
Customs - Via Valfonda, 25 - ☎ 214316
Heart Emergency (Mobile Coronary Unit) - ☎ 214444
Radio-Taxi - ☎ 4390-4798
Railways Central Switchboard - ☎ 2767
Railways Information - ☎ 278785
Night-time and Holiday Medical Assistance - ☎ 477891
Ambulances (Misericordia) - ☎ 212222
Ambulances (Fratellanza Militare) - ☎ 215555
Railway Police - ☎ 212296
Motorway Police - ☎ 577777
Police Headquarters (Questura) - ☎ 49771
Fire Brigade - ☎ 222222
City Police (Railway Station) - ☎ 212290
City Police (Emergency Squad) - ☎ 352141
City Police - (Palazzo Vecchio) - ☎ 284926
City Police - (Via delle Terme) - ☎ 292012

TOURIST INFORMATION

Ente Provinciale per il Turismo
(Provincial Tourist Information)
Via Manzoni, 16 - ☎ 2478141
Azienda Autonoma di Turismo
(Autonomous Tourist Office)
Via Tornabuoni, 15 - ☎ 216544
Automobile Club di Firenze
(Florentine branch of the Automobile Club)
V.le Amendola, 36 - ☎ 27841
Emergency Motorway Assistance - ☎ 666500

LOST PROPERTY OFFICE

All lost property is taken to the Municipal office at Via Circondaria, 19 - ☎ 367943, whether delivered to the Police, to the Carabinieri or to the Railway Police. Property left in taxis can be recovered from the City Police or, after two or three days, from the Lost Property Office.

CONSULATES

Austria - V. dei Servi, 9 - ☎ 215352
Belgium - V. dei Conti, 4 - ☎ 294276-282094
Bolivia - V. Torre del Gallo, 24 - ☎ 220017
Cile - V. Alamanni, 25 - ☎ 214131
Costa Rica - V. Giambologna, 10 - ☎ 573603
Denmark - V. dei Servi, 13 - ☎ 211007
Federal Republic of Germany - B.go SS. Apostoli 22 - ☎ 294722
Finland - V. Strozzi 6 - ☎ 293228
France - P.zza Ognissanti 2 - ☎ 213509
Great Britain - Lung.no Corsini, 2 - ☎ 284133
Haiti - V. Cerretani, 2 - ☎ 282683
Honduras - V. de' Bardi, 30 - ☎ 282219
Malta - V.le Gramsci, 42 - ☎ 242958
Mexico - V.le Belfiore 14 - ☎ 472466
Netherlands - V. Cavour 81 - ☎ 475249
Norway - V. Piana 8/F - ☎ 2280316
Panama - V. Tornabuoni, 10 - ☎ 216762
Peru - V. della Mattonaia, 17 - ☎ 672345
Principality of Monaco - V. Cherubini, 18 - ☎ 587897
San Marino - V. Roma, 3 - ☎ 210864
Spain - P.zza dei Saltarelli, 1 - ☎ 212173
Sweden - V. della Scala, 4 - ☎ 296865
Switzerland - P.le Galileo, 5 - ☎ 222434
United States of America - Lung.no Vespucci, 38 - ☎ 298276
Venezuela - V. Giambologna, 10 - ☎ 588082

TRAVEL AGENCIES

A.B.C. · Viaggi e vacanze
Via dei Banchi, 25r · ☎ 283825
American Express
Via Guicciardini, 49r · ☎ 278751
Arno Travel
Piazza Ottaviani, 7r · ☎ 295251
Chiariva
Via Vacchereccia, 26r · ☎ 211968
Cit
Via Cavour, 53/r · ☎ 294310
Eyre e Humbert
Piazza Rucellai, 4/7r · ☎ 262251
Globus Viaggi
S. Trinità, 2r · ☎ 214992
Intertravel
Via Lamberti, 39/41r · 265141
Italturist
Por S. Maria, 4 · ☎ 210853
Lazzi Express
Piazza Stazione, 47r · ☎ 294178
Melià
Via Cavour, 63r · ☎ 219190
Newtours
Via G. Monaco, 20/a · ☎ 475303
Pentatours
Via Sassetti, 19r · ☎ 264251
Roller Tours
Piazza Stazione, 23r · ☎ 298158
Saturnia Tours
Borgognissanti, 75r · ☎ 282100
Tecnotravel
Via dell'Oriuolo, 50r · ☎ 217555
Universalturismo
Via degli Speziali, 7r · American Express Agent ·
☎ 217241
Wagons-Lits Turismo
Via del Giglio, 27r · ☎ 218851

CHEMISTS OPEN
ALL NIGHT
From 20.00 to 9.00

Bargioni
Via G.P. Orsini, 107/r · ☎ 6811616
Codecà
Via Ginori, 50/r · ☎ 210849
Comunale N° 5
P.za dell'Isolotto, 5 · ☎ 703191
Comunale N° 6
V.le Calatafimi, 6/r · ☎ 600945
Comunale N° 8
V.le Guidoni, 8/r · ☎ 415546
Del Galluzzo
Via Senese, 206/208/r · ☎ 2049217

Della Nave
P.za delle Cure, 1/2 · ☎ 573717
Di Rifredi
P.za Dalmazia, 24/r · ☎ 473875
Morelli
Via G.P. Orsini, 27/r · ☎ 6812145
Mungai
Via Starnina, 41/r · ☎ 708595
Paglicci
Via della Scala, 49/r · ☎ 215612
Paoletti
Via di Brozzi, 282/a/b · ☎ 380248

HOSPITALS

Arcispedale di S. Maria Nuova
(Largest Central General Hospital)
P.zza S. Maria Nuova, 1 · ☎ 27581
Ospedale Anna Meyer
(Children's Hospital)
Via L. Giordano, 13 · ☎ 43991
Policlinico di Careggi
(Major University Hospital)
Vl. Morgagni, 85 · ☎ 43991
Nuovo Ospedale di San Giovanni di Dio
(Large General Hospital of Recent Construction)
Via Torregalli, 3 · ☎ 27661
Ospedale Santa Maria Annunziata
(Newly built General Hospital)
Via dell'Antella - Antella · ☎ 27941
Centro Traumatologico Ortopedico
(Traumatological and Orthopedic Centre),
L.go P. Palagi, 1 · ☎ 413645-415441-416781
Istituto Ortopedico Toscano
(Tuscan Orthopedic Institute)
V.le Michelangiolo, 41 · ☎ 6813811

MUSEUMS AND GALLERIES

Anthropological Museum
Via Proconsolo, 12 · ☎ 296449
1st and 3rd Sun. of the Month from 9.00-13.00
Archaeological Museum
Via della Colonna, 36 · ☎ 2478641
Week. 9.00-14.00 · Hols. 9.00-13.00
Closed Mon.
Bardini Museum and Corsi Gallery
Piazza de' Mozzi · ☎ 296749
Week. 9.00-14.00 · Hols. 8.00-13.00
Closed Wed.
Bargello
Via del Proconsolo, 4 · ☎ 210801
Week. 9.00-14.00 · Hols. 9.00-13.00
Closed Mon.

Botanical Museum and Gardens
Via Micheli, 3 · ☎ 284696
Mon. Wed. Fri. 9.00-12.00.
Brancacci Chapel
Piazza del Carmine · ☎ 212331
Every day 7.00-12.00 · 15.30-19.00
Buonarroti House
Via Ghibellina, 70 · ☎ 241752
Week. 9.00-14.00 · Hols. 9.00-13.00
Closed Tue.
Cloisters of Santa Maria Novella
Piazza S. Maria Novella · ☎ 282187
Week. 9.00-14.00 · Hols. 8.00-13.00
Closed Fri.
Costumes Museum
Palazzo Pitti · ☎ 294279
Week. 9.00-14.00 · Hols. 9.00-13.00
Closed Mon.
Dante's House
Via S. Margherita, 1 · ☎ 283343
Week. 9.30-12.30 · 15.30-18.30 · Hols. 9.30-12.30
Closed Wed.
Florence as it was and Garden of the Oblates
Via Oriuolo, 4 · ☎ 217305
Week. 9.00-14.00 · Hols. 8.00-13.00
Closed Thur.
Gallery of Modern Art
Palazzo Pitti · ☎ 287096
Week. 9.00-14.00 · Hols. 9.00-13.00
Closed Mon.
Gallery of Plaster casts of the Institute of Art.
P.le di Porta Romana, 9 · ☎ 220521
Open (8.30-12.00, upon request) from Mon. to Sat.
Gallery of the Academy
Via Ricasoli, 60 · ☎ 214375
Week. 9.00-14.00 · Hols. 9.00-13.00
Closed Mon.
Horne Museum
Via de' Benci, 6 · ☎ 244661
Week. 9.00-13.00 · Closed Sun.
Hospital of the Innocents
Piazza SS. Annunziata, 12 · ☎ 243670
Week. 9.00 -14.00 · Hols. 8.00-13.00
Closed Wed.
Jewish Museum of Florence
Via Farini, 4 · ☎ 245252
May-Sept.: Sun. Mon. Wed. (9.00-18.00)
Tue. Thur. (9.00-13.00). Oct.-Apr.: Sun.-Thur. (9.00-13.00).
La Specola Museum
Via Romana, 17 · ☎ 222451
Zoology: Tue. (9.00-12.30) - Sun. (9.00-12.00)
Waxworks: Sat. (14.00-17.00: winter)
(15.00-18.00: summer.
Medici Chapels
Piazza Madonna · ☎ 213206

Week. 9.00-14.00 · Hols. 9.00-13.00
Closed Mon.
Medici-Riccardi Palace
Via Cavour, 1 · ☎ 2760
Week. 9.00-12.00 · 15.00-17.00 · Hols. 9.00-12.00
Closed Wed.
Modern Art Collection (A. della Ragione)
Piazza Signoria, 5 · ☎ 283078
Week. 9.00-14.00 · Hols. 8.00-13.00
Closed Tue.
Museum of Mineralogy
Via La Pira, 4 · ☎ 287140
Week. 9.00-13.00 · Closed Weekends and Hols.
Museum of St. Mark
Piazza S. Marco, 1 · ☎ 210741
Week. 9.00-14.00 · Hols. 9.00-13.00
Closed Mon.
Museum of the Ancient Florentine Home
Piazza Davanzati · ☎ 216518
Week. 9.00-13.15 · Hols. 9.00-12.15
Closed Mon.
Opera di Santa Maria del Fiore Museum
Piazza Duomo, 9 · ☎ 213229
Week. 9.00-18.00
Hols. 9.00-13.00
Opificio delle Pietre Dure (Semi-precious Stone Inlay Laboratories)
Via Alfani, 78 · ☎ 210102
Week. 9.00-13.00 · Closed Sun.
Palatine Gallery
Palazzo Pitti · ☎ 216673
Week. 9.00-14.00 · Hols. 9.00-13.00
Closed Mon.
Palazzo Vecchio and Monumental Apartments
Piazza Signoria, ☎ 27681
Week. 9.00-19.00 · Hols. 8.00-13.00
Closed Sat.
Paleontology Museum
Via La Pira, 4 · ☎ 262711
Mon. 14.00-18.00 · Thur.-Sat. 9.00-13.00
Ist. Sun. of the Month (excl. July, Aug. Sept.) 9.30-12.30
Closed Hols.
Porcelain Museum
Boboli Gardens (Palazzo Pitti) · ☎ 287976
Tue. Thur. Sat.: 9.00-14.00
Primo Conti Museum
Le Coste - Via Dupré 18, Fiesole · ☎ 597095
10.00-13.00 · 15.00-18.00 · Closed Sun. and Hols
«Royal» Apartments
Palazzo Pitti · ☎ 210323
Week. 9.00-14.00 · Hols. 9.00-13.00
Closed Mon.
Santa Croce Museum
Piazza S. Croce, 16 · ☎ 244619
Open: 9.00-12.30 · 15.00-17.00 · Closed Wed.

Science History Institute and Museum
P.zza Giudici, 1 · ☎ 293493
Hols. 9.30-13.00
Mon. Wed. Fri. 9.30-13.30 · 14.00-16.00
Closed Sat. and Hols.

Silver Museum
Palazzo Pitti · ☎ 212557
Week. 9.00-14.00 · Hols. 9.00-13.00
Closed Mon.

Stibbert Museum
Via Stibbert, 26 · ☎ 475520
Week. 9.00-14.00 · Hols. 9.00-12.30
Closed Thur.

Uffizi Gallery
Loggiato degli Uffizi, 6 · ☎ 218341
Week. 9.00-19.00 · Hols. 9.00-13.00
Closed Mon.

FRESCOED HALLS OR CLOISTERS

Ghirlandaio Refectory
Borgognissanti, 42 · ☎ 296802
Open every day 9.00-12.00 · 16.00-18.00

Perugino Crucifixion
Borgo Pinti, 58 · 9.00-12.00 · 17.00-19.00

The Foligno Conservatory
Via Faenza, 42 · ☎ 286982
Hols. 9.00-12.00 · Closed Weekdays
Now closed for restoration

Refectory of St. Apollonia
Via XXVII Aprile, 1 · ☎ 287074
Timetable 9.00-14.00 · Hols. 9.00-13.00
Closed Mon.

Refectory of Andrea del Sarto
Via S. Salvi, 16 · ☎ 677570
Timetable: 9.00-14.00
Closed Mon.

The Scalzo Cloister
Via Cavour, 69 · ☎ 472812
Timetable: 9.00-14.00 · Hols. 9.00-13.00
Closed Mon.

Refectory of Santo Spirito
Piazza S. Spirito · ☎ 287043
Open Weekdays 9-14 · Hols. 8.00-13.00
Closed Mon.

NON-CATHOLIC PLACES OF WORSHIP

American Episcopal Church, St. James
Via B. Rucellai, 9 · ☎ 294417 · Timetable of
Services: Sun. 9.30, 11.00.

Christian Adventist Church
Via Guelfa, 12 · ☎ 287340 · Timetable of Services: Sat. 9.30: Biblical Study 10.30 Service · Via
del Pergolino, 12 · ☎ 412014 · Timetable: Saturday
School 9.30 · Service 11.

Church of England
Via Maggio, 16 · ☎ 294764 · Timetablel of Services: Sun. 9.00 (Spoken) and 10.30 (Sung) 2nd Sun
of the Month only 9.00 (at 10.30 in St. Peter's in
Siena). · Wed. 10.00 · Fri. 20.00.

Church of Evangelical Brotherhood
Via Vigna Vecchia 15/17 · ☎ 217236 · Sun. 10.15 ·
Thur. 20.30.

Evangelical Baptists
Borgo Ognissanti, 6 · ☎ 210537 · Timetable: Sun.
11 · Service; Mon. 17.00 Prayer.

Evangelical Lutheran Church
Lungarno Torrigiani, 11 · ☎ 296375 · Timetable of
Services: Sun. 10.00.

Evangelical Valdese
Place of Worship: Via Micheli, on the corner of
Via Lamarmora · ☎ 2477800 · Sunday Service:
10.30 · 11.15 · Women's Union: Via Manzoni, 21 ·
Wed. 16.00 · Youth Catechumen Group and
Sunday School: Via Manzoni, 21 · Sat. 15.30.

Jewish Community
Via L. Farini, 4 · ☎ 245252-245253 · Weekdays
and Half-Hols. (incl. Fri.) Shachrit 7.30; for further information phone 245252.
Visits to Synagogue from 9.00 until half and hour
before functions.

Russian Orthodox Church
Via Leone X, 8 · ☎ 490148 · Timetable of Servi-
ces: Third Sun. of the Month and Main Liturgical
Festivities: 10.30 · Orthodox Rite in Russian.

IInd WORLD WAR CEMETERIES

American War Cemetery
About 8 Kms south of Florence towards Siena,
near Falciani. Open from 8.00 to 17.00 (Mon. to
Fri.) and 9.30 to 17.00 Sat. · ☎ 2020020

British Commonwealth War Cemetery
About 7 Kms east of Florence, towards Arezzo;
road Nr. 67, near Girone. Open every day (9.00-
17.00) Sun.: 9.00-13.00.

German War Cemetery
Near Traversa just beyond the Futa pass; ☎
815248. Open every day from 8.30 to 12.00 and
from 14.00 to 19.00.

**South African War Cemetery of Castiglione dei
Pepoli.**
About 48 Kms from Florence, towards Bologna, at
Castiglione dei Pepoli. The road rises from
Prato, along the Bisenzio valley. The cemetery is
250 ms. left of the road just outside Castiglione.

LIBRARIES

Archives of the Opera del Duomo
P. Duomo, 8 · ☎ 213229
Open: 9.00-12.30 · Closed Sat.
American Library
Via S. Gallo, 10 · ☎ 296114
Open: 9.00-12.00 · Closed Sat.
Biblioteca Comunale Centrale (Central Municipal Lib.)
Via S. Egidio, 21 · ☎ 282863
Open: 9.00-19.00 · Sat. 9.00-13.00
Biblioteca dell'Orticoltura (Orticultural Lib.)
Via Vittorio Emanuele, 1 · ☎ 486743
Open: 15.00-19.30 · Sat. 9.00-13.00
«P. Thouar» Library
Via Mazzetta, 10 · ☎ 298740
Open: 14.30-19.30 · Sat. 8.30-13.30
Biblioteca Medicea Laurenziana (Medici Lib.)
Piazza S. Lorenzo, 9 · ☎ 210760
Open: 8.00-14.00
Biblioteca del Collegio Teologico dei Carmelitani Scalzi (Theological College of the Carmel Order)
Via S. Matteo in Arcetri, 18 · ☎ 220029
Open: 9.00-12.00 · 16.00-18.30 · Closed Sat.
Library of the Cherubini Music Academy
Via Alfani, 80 · ☎ 292180 · Open: 9.00-12.00
Historical Archives of the Communal Offices
Via dell'Oriolo, 33 · ☎ 2340383
Open: 8.30-13.30
Library of the Convent of St. Mark's
Via Cavour, 56 · ☎ 287628 · Open Thur.: 8.30-12.00 · 16.00-19.00
Library of the G.P. Vieusseux Scientific-Literary Cabinet
P.zza Strozzi, Palazzo Strozzi · ☎ 215990
Open: 9.00-13.00 · 15.00-19.00 · Sat. 9.00-13.00
Library of the Economic-Agrarian Academy of the Georgofili
Logge degli Uffizi · ☎ 213360 · Open: 15.30-19.00
Biblioteca dell'Accademia Italiana di Scienze Forestali
P. Edison, 11 · ☎ 570348 · Open: 9.30-12.30
Library of the Accademia Toscana di Scienze e Lettere «La Colombaria»
Via S. Egidio, 21 · ☎ 296628
Open: 16.00-18.00 · Closed Sat.
Library of the Librarian Resources Service
Via G. Modena, 13 · ☎ 576779 · Open: 9.00-13.00
Information on all the libraries in town.
State Archives Library · Loggiato degli Uffizi
☎ 211629 · Open: 8.45-13.40 · Sat. 8.45-12.40
Library of the Italian Dante Society
Via Arte della Lana, 1 · ☎ 294580
Open: 15.30-19.00 · Sat. Closed.

Library of the Soprintendenza per i Beni Artistici e Storici di Firenze (Artistic and Historical Resources Dept.)
Via della Ninna, 5 · ☎ 218341 · Open: 9.00-13.00
Library of the Overseas Agronomy Institute
Via Cocchi, 4 · ☎ 573201 · Open: 8.30-13.30
British Institute Library
Lungarno Guicciardini, 9 · ☎ 284031
Open: 9.45-12.45 · 15.15-19.15 · Sat. closed.
Library of the Etruscan and Italic Studies Institute
Via della Pergola, 65 · ☎ 2478641 · Open 8.30-13.00
Library of the National Institute of Renaissance Studies
Pal. Strozzi · P.zza Strozzi · ☎ 287728
Open: 9-13
Library of the Science History Institute and Museum
P. dei Giudici, 1 · ☎ 293493 · Open: 9.00-13.00 · 16.00-18.00 · Sat. 9.00-13.00
Library of the French Institute
Piazza Ognissanti, 2 · ☎ 298902
Open: 10.00-13.00 15.00-18.00 · Sat. closed.
Library of the «Stensen» Institute
Viale Don Minzoni, 25 · ☎ 576551 · Open: 9.00-12.00 · 16.00-19.00 · Sat. Closed.
Library of the German History of Art Institute
Via Giusti, 44 · ☎ 2479161 · Open: 9.00-19.00
Sat. closed.
Marucelliana Library
Via Cavour, 43 · ☎ 210602
Open: 9.00-13.00 · 15.00-20.00 · Sat. 9.00-12.30
Library of the Dutch University Institute
Via Torricelli, 5 · ☎ 221612
Open: 9.00-13.00 · 14.00-18.00 · Sat. Closed.
Biblioteca Nazionale Centrale (Central National Library)
P.zza Cavalleggeri, 1 · ☎ 244443
Open: 9.00-18.45 · Sat. 9.00-13.00
Riccardiana Library
Via dei Ginori, 10 · ☎ 212586 · Open: 8.00-14.00

BANKS

Working Hours: 8.20-13.20; 14.45-15.45 · Closed Sat. and Sun.

American Service Bank
Via della Vigna Nuova, 2r · ☎ 218141
Banca C. Steinhauslin
Via Sassetti, 4 · ☎ 27621
Banca Commerciale Italiana
Via Strozzi, 8 · ☎ 27851
Banca D'America e D'Italia
Via Strozzi, 16 · ☎ 278721

Banca D'Italia
Via dell'Oriuolo, 37/39 · ☎ 218741
Banca Mercantile
Piazza Davanzati, 3 · ☎ 2765
Banca Nazionale del Lavoro
Via Strozzi, 1 · ☎ 27931
Banca Nazionale dell'Agricoltura
Via Ricasoli, 8/b · ☎ 264121
Banca Nazionale delle Comunicazioni
Piazza della Repubblica, 4 · ☎ 294776
Banca Popolare di Novara
Piazza dell'Unità Italiana, 4 · ☎ 295253
Banca Toscana
Via del Corso, 4 · ☎ 287018
Banco di Napoli
Via Cavour, 20/22/24 · ☎ 278761
Banco di Roma
Via Vecchietti, 5 · ☎ 2782
Banco di Sicilia
Piazza della Repubblica, 1/a · ☎ 27901
Cassa di Risparmio di Firenze
Via Bufalini, 6 · ☎ 27801
Credito Artigiano
Via Boni, 1 · ☎ 218641
Credito Italiano
Via Vecchietti, 11 · ☎ 27971
Federico del Vecchio
Via Dei Banchi, 5 · ☎ 282241
Istituto Bancario Italiano
Lungarno Corsini, 2 · ☎ 278681
Istituto Bancario S. Paolo di Torino
Via Vecchietti, 22/r · ☎ 264061
Istituto Mobiliare Italiano
Piazza Savonarola, 22 · ☎ 579486
Monte dei Paschi di Siena
Via dei Pecori, 6/8 · ☎ 49711
Nuovo Banco Ambrosiano
Via delle Farine, 1 (Corner of P.za Signoria) · ☎ 264091

CAMPING SITES - YOUTH HOSTELS

Autosole
Via Vitt. Emanuele, 11 - Calenzano (FI) · ☎ 882391
90 tent areas
Italiani e Stranieri
Viale Michelangiolo, 80 · ☎ 6811977
500 tent areas
Panoramico
Via Peramonda · ☎ 599069 (Fiesole)
480 tent areas
Villa Camerata
Viale A. Righi, 2/4 · ☎ 610300 · 180 tent areas
Ostello della Gioventù Villa Camerata
Viale Righi, 2 · ☎ 601451

Santa Monaca
Via S. Monaca, 6 · ☎ 268338
Villa Favard · Parking area
Via Rocca Tedalda · Bus Nr. 14-62 (Open in Summer)

HOTELS

★ ★ ★ ★ ★

Excelsior Italie · Piazza Ognissanti 3 · ☎ 264201
Grand Hotel · Piazza Ognissanti, 1 · ☎ 278781
Grand Hotel Villa Cora · Viale Machiavelli, 18 · ☎ 2298451
Regency Umbria · Piazza M. D'Azeglio, 3 · ☎ 245247
Savoy · Piazza della Repubblica, 7 · ☎ 283313
Villa La Massa · Candeli · Bagno a Ripoli · ☎ 630051
Villa Medici · Via Il Prato, 42 · ☎ 261331

★ ★ ★ ★

Alexander · Viale Guidoni, 101 · ☎ 4378951
Anglo-American Hotel Regina · Via Garibaldi, 9 · ☎ 282114
Astoria Etap · Via del Giglio, 9 · ☎ 298095
Augustus · Vicolo dell'Oro, 5 · ☎ 283054
Baglioni · Piazza Unità Italiana, 6 · ☎ 218441
Crest Hotel · Viale Europa, 205 · ☎ 686841
Croce di Malta · Via della Scala, 7 · ☎ 282600
De la Ville · Piazza Antinori, 1 · ☎ 261805
Della Signoria · Via delle Terme, 1 · ☎ 214530
Executive · Via Curtatone, 5 · ☎ 217451
Grand Hotel Majestic · Via del Melarancio, 1 · ☎ 264021
Grand Hotel Minerva · P.za S. Maria Novella, 16 · ☎ 284555
Jolly Carlton · Piazza Vittorio Veneto, 4-A · ☎ 2770
Kraft · Via Solferino, 2 · ☎ 284273
Laurus · Via Cerretani, 8 · ☎ 261752
Londra · Via Jacopo da Diacceto, 18/20 · ☎ 262791
Lungarno · Borgo S. Jacopo, 14 · ☎ 264211
Michelangelo · Viale F.lli Rosselli, 2 · ☎ 278711
Milano Terminus · Via Cerretani, 10 · ☎ 283372
Mirage · Via Baracca, 231 · ☎ 352011
Monginevro · Via di Novoli, 59 · ☎ 431441
Montebello Splendid · Via Montebello, 60 · ☎ 298051
Nord Florence · Via Baracca, 199 · ☎ 431151
Park Palace · Piazzale Galileo, 5 · ☎ 222431

Plaza & Lucchesi · Lung. della Zecca Vecchia, 38 · ☎ 264141
Principe · Lung. Vespucci, 34 · ☎ 284848
Queen Palace Hotel · Via Solferino, 5 · ☎ 296818
Villa Carlotta · Via M. di Lando, 3 · ☎ 220530
Ville sull'Arno · Lung. Colombo, 1 · 670971

★ ★ ★

Adriatico · Via Maso Finiguerra, 9 · ☎ 261781
Albion · Via Il Prato, 22r · ☎ 214171
Ambasciatori · Via L. Alamani, 3 · ☎ 287421
Annalena · Via Romana, 34 · ☎ 222402
Argentina · Via Curtatone, 12 · ☎ 298203
Ariete · Via Magenta, 11 · ☎ 211509
Astor · Viale Milton, 41 · ☎ 483391
Balestri · Piazza Mentana, 7 · ☎ 294242
Basilea · Via Guelfa, 41 · ☎ 214587
Beacci Tornabuoni · Via Tornabuoni, 3 · ☎ 212645
Bonciani · Via Panzani, 17 · ☎ 210039
Calzaiuoli · Via Calzaiuoli, 6 · ☎ 212456
Capitol · Viale Amendola, 34 · ☎ 675201
Caravel · Via L. Alamanni, 9 · ☎ 217651
Castri · Piazza Indipendenza, 7 · ☎ 496412
Cavour · Via del Proconsolo, 3 · ☎ 287102
Cellai · Via XXVII Aprile, 14 · ☎ 489291
Columbus · Lung. Colombo, 22 · ☎ 677251
Concorde · Viale L. Gori, 10 · ☎ 373551
Continental · Lung. Acciaiuoli, 2 · ☎ 282392
Corallo · Via Nazionale, 22a · ☎ 499304
Da Verrazzano · Via di Bellariva, 18 · ☎ 679766
David · Viale Michelangelo, 1 · ☎ 6811696
De La Pace · Via Lamarmora, 28 · ☎ 577343
Duomo · Piazza Duomo, 1 · ☎ 219922
Embassy House · Via Nazionale, 23 · ☎ 262266
Fleming · Viale Guidoni, 87 · ☎ 4376331
Golf · Viale F.lli Rosselli, 56 · ☎ 293088
Helvetia & Bristol · Via de' Pescioni, 2 · ☎ 287814
Hermitage · Vicolo Marzio, 1 · ☎ 287216
Jennings Riccioli · C. Tintori, 7 · ☎ 244751
La Residenza · Via Tornabuoni, 8 · ☎ 284197
Le due Fontane · P.zza SS. Annunziata, 14 · ☎ 210185
Leonardo da Vinci · Via G. Monaco, 12 · ☎ 474352
Mediterraneo · Lung. del Tempio, 44 · ☎ 672241
Paris · Via de' Banchi, 2 · ☎ 280281
Pendini · Via Strozzi, 2 · ☎ 211170
Porta Rossa · Via Porta Rossa, 19 · ☎ 287551
Quisiana & Ponte Vecchio · Lung. Archibusieri, 4 · ☎ 216692
Rapallo · Via S. Caterina d'Alessandria, 7 · ☎ 472412
Residence Firenze Nova · Via Panciatichi, 51 · ☎ 477851

Ritz · Lung. Zecca Vecchia, 24 · ☎ 671651
River · Lung. della Zecca Vecchia, 18 · ☎ 677951
Rivoli · Via della Scala, 33 · ☎ 216988
Roma Pietrobelli · Piazza S.M. Novella, 8 · ☎ 210366
Via Azalee · Viale F.lli Rosselli, 44 · ☎ 214242
Villa Belvedere · Via Senese, 93 · ☎ 222501
Villa Betania · Viale Poggio Imperiale, 23 · ☎ 220532
Villa Le Rondini · Via Bolognese Vecchia, 224 · ☎ 400081
Villa Liberty · Viale Michelangelo, 40 · ☎ 6810581

★ ★

Arizona · Via Farini, 2 · ☎ 245321
Arno Bellariva · Lung. del Tempio, 16 · ☎ 663509
Ascot · Via Nazionale, 8a · ☎ 284171
Benvenuti · Via Cavour, 112 · ☎ 572141
Boboli · Via Romana, 63 · ☎ 227169
Bretagna · Lungarno Corsini, 6 · ☎ 263618
Byron · Via della Scala, 49 · ☎ 216700
Casa del Lago · Lungarno Vespucci, 58 · ☎ 216141
Consigli · Lungarno Vespucci, 50 · ☎ 214172
Corona · Via Nazionale, 14 · ☎ 278631
Costantini · Via Calzaiuoli, 13 · ☎ 215128
Crocini · Corso Italia, 28 · ☎ 212905
Delle Nazioni · Via Alamanni, 15 · ☎ 283575
Derby · Via Nazionale, 35 · ☎ 219308
Europa · Via Cavour, 14 · ☎ 210361
Madrid · Via della Scala, 59 · ☎ 282776
Medici · Via de' Medici, 6 · ☎ 216202
Melagnano · Via Maso Finiguerra · ☎ 214013
Nuovo Atlantico · Via Nazionale, 10 · ☎ 218622
Pagnini · Via Montebello, 40 · ☎ 261238
Patrizia · Via Montebello, 7 · ☎ 282314
Primavera · Via Maso Finiguerra, 12r · ☎ 287072
Rigatti · Lungarno Diaz, 2 · ☎ 213022
Versailles · Via Martelli, 3 · ☎ 287575

RESTAURANTS

Acqua al due (Chi-inn) · Via Acqua, 2r · ☎ 284170
Acquerello · Via Ghibellina, 156r · ☎ 2340554
Alfredo sull'Arno · Via dei Bardi 46r · ☎ 283808
Alle Murate · Via Ghibellina, 52r · ☎ 240618
Antico Crespino · Largo Fermi, 15 · ☎ 221155
Antico Fattore · Via Lambertesca, 1r · ☎ 261215
Armando · Bg. Ognissanti, 140r · ☎ 216219
Baldini · Via Il Prato, 96r · ☎ 287663
Barone · Via Romana 123r · ☎ 220585

Buca Lapi · Via Trebbio, 1r · ☎ 213768
Buca Mario · P. Ottaviani, 16r · ☎ 214179
Buca dell'Orafo · Via Girolami, 28r · ☎ 213619
Cammillo · Borgo S. Jacopo, 57r · ☎ 212427
Campidoglio · Via del Campidoglio, 8r · ☎ 287770
Cantinetta Antinori · Piazza Antinori, 3 · ☎ 292234
Celestino · Piazza S. Felicita, 4r · ☎ 292185-296574
Coco Lezzone · Via Parioncino, 26r · ☎ 287178
Da Noi · Via Fiesolana, 46r · ☎ 242917
Da Zi Rosa · Via dei Fossi, 12r · ☎ 287062
Delfina · Via della Chiesa - Artimino · ☎ 8718074
Dino · Via Ghibellina, 51r · ☎ 241452
Don Chisciotte · Via C. Ridolfi, 4-6r · ☎ 475430
Drago Verde · Via del Leone, 50 · ☎ 224002
Enoteca · Via Ghibellina, 87 · ☎ 242777
Harry's Bar · Lungarno A. Vespucci, 22 · ☎ 296700
I due «G» · Via Cennini, 7 · ☎ 218623
Il Barretto · American Bar Grill (ex The Octopus Club) · Via del Parione, 50 · ☎ 294122
Il Barrino · Via De' Biffi, 2r · ☎ 215180
Il Caminetto · Via dello Studio, 34r · ☎ 296274
Il Cenacolo · Bg. Ognissanti, 34 · ☎ 219493
Il Cestello · Roof Garden Hotel Excelsior · ☎ 264201
Il Cibreo · Via dei Macci, 118 · ☎ 2341100
Il Gourmet · Via Il Prato, 68r · ☎ 294766
Il Pavone · Via Cavour, 108r · ☎ 295210
Il Profeta · Bg. Ognissanti, 93r · ☎ 212265
Il Verrocchio · Hotel Villa La Massa · Via La Massa - Candeli (FI) · ☎ 630051-2
La Capannina di Sante · P.zza Ravenna · ☎ 688345
La Galleria · Via Guicciardini, 48r · ☎ 218541
La Greppia · Lung. Ferrucci, 4 · ☎ 6812341
La Grotta Guelfa · Via Pellicceria, 5r · ☎ 210042
La Loggia · Piazzale Michelangelo · ☎ 287032
La Posta · Via Pellicceria, 28r · ☎ 212701
La Vineria · P.za Ghiberti, 35 · ☎ 2341100
Latini · Via Palchetti, 6r · ☎ 210916
Le Cave di Maiano · Via delle Cave, 16 - Fiesole · ☎ 59133
Le Fonticine · Via Nazionale, 76r · ☎ 282106
Le Lance · Via Mantellini, 19b · ☎ 599090
Le Rampe · Viale Poggi, 1 · ☎ 6811891
Leo in Santa Croce · Via Torta, 7r · ☎ 210829
Lorenzaccio · Via B. Rucellai, 1a · ☎ 217100
Lo Strettoio · Via Serpiolle, 7 · ☎ 403044
Lume di Candela · Via Terme, 23r · ☎ 294566
Mamma Gina · Borgo S. Jacopo, 37r · ☎ 296009
Monna Lisa · Music Hall Via Faenza, 4 · ☎ 210298

Natale · Lungarno Acciaiuoli, 80r · ☎ 213968
Oliviero · Via delle Terme, 51r · ☎ 287643
Omero · Pian dei Giullari, 11 · ☎ 220053
Osteria N. 1 · Via del Moro, 22 · ☎ 284897
Otello · Via Orti Oricellari, 28r · ☎ 215819
Ottorino · Via delle Oche, 12-16r · ☎ 218747
Paoli · Via Tavolini, 12r · ☎ 216215
Pierot · Piazza T. Gaddi, 25r · ☎ 702100
Pop inn · P.za S. Marco, 7 · ☎ 210438
Sabatini · Via Panzani, 41-43r · ☎ 211559
Sostanza · Via Porcellana, 25r · ☎ 212691
Taverna del Bronzino · Via delle Ruote, 25-27r · ☎ 495220
Tredici Gobbi · Via Porcellana, 9r · ☎ 298769
Villa Vecchia · Via della Lupaia, 35 - Pratolino · ☎ 409246

PIZZA RESTAURANTS

Borgo Antico
P.za S. Spirito, 6r · ☎ 210437
Danny Rock
Via Pandolfini, 13 · ☎ 2340307
I Tarocchi
Via Renai, 12r · ☎ 217850
La Bussola
Via Porta Rossa, 58r · ☎ 293376
La Greppia
Lung. Ferrucci, 4/8 · ☎ 6812341
La Lampara
Via Nazionale, 36r · ☎ 215164
Nuti
Borgo S. Lorenzo, 39r · ☎ 210410
Osteria Il Gatto e la Volpe (2)
Via Ghibellina, 151r · ☎ 263264
Pitt Stop Pizza
Via F. Corridoni, 30r · ☎ 472089
Pizzeus
Viale Gramsci, 9/11r · ☎ 672980
Pop inn
P.za S. Marco, 7 · ☎ 210438
San Domenico
P.za S. Domenico, 11 - Fiesole · ☎ 59182
Yellow
Via Proconsolo, 39r · ☎ 211766

CHINESE RESTAURANTS

China Town · Via Vecchietti, 6-8-10r · ☎ 294470
Fior di Loto · Via dei Servi, 35r · ☎ 298235
Il Mandarino · Via Condotta, 17 · ☎ 296130
Nanchino · Via De' Cerchi, 40r · ☎ 213142
Peking · Via del Melarancio, 21 · ☎ 282922

Florence by night

NIGHT CLUBS

Central Park
Via Fosso Macinante, 13
Parco Cascine · ☎ 356723
(Open from May to September)
River Club
Lungarno Corsini, 8 · ☎ 282465

PIANO BARS

Caffè
Piazza Pitti, 9 · ☎ 296241
Chapeau
Via Verdi, 57-59r · ☎ 298738
Full-up
Via della Vigna Vecchia, 21 · ☎ 293006
Il Barretto · American Bar Grill (ex The Octopus Club)
Via del Parione, 50 · ☎ 294122
Jackie O'
Via dell'Erta Canina, 42b · ☎ 216146
Loggia Tornaquinci
Via Tornabuoni, 6 · ☎ 219148

Oliviero
Via delle Terme, 51/r · ☎ ☎ 287643
Tabasco (Gay)
Piazza S. Cecilia, 3 · ☎ 213000
Tabeta
Vicolo dell'Oro · ☎ 263446

DISCOTÈQUES

Chalet Fontana
Via S. Leonardo, 8r · ☎ 221187
Chapeau
Via Verdi, 57-59r · ☎ 298738
Divina
Borgo Albizi, 66 · ☎ 214406
(Open July-August)
Full-Up
Via della Vigna Vecchia, 21 · ☎ 293006
Jackie O'
Via dell'Erta Canina, 42b · ☎ 216146
La Cave
Hotel Villa La Massa · Via La Massa · Candeli (FI) · ☎ 630051-2
Space Electronic
Via Palazzuolo, 37 · ☎ 293082
Tiffany
Lungarno Colombo, 23 · ☎ 676912
Yab Yum
Via Sassetti, 5 · ☎ 225657

CONTENTS

Translation revised by ROSALYND PIO